Grounded Theory in Management Research

Karen Locke

SAGE Publications
London • Thousand Oaks • New Delhi

First published 2001

SAGE Publications Ltd
6 Bonhill Street
London EC2A 4PU

SAGE Publications Inc
2455 Teller Road
Thousand Oaks, California 91320

SAGE Publications India Pvt Ltd
32, M-Block Market
Greater Kailash – I
New Delhi 110 048

British Library Cataloguing in Publication data

A catalogue record for this book is available from the British Library.

ISBN 0 7619 6427 4
ISBN 0 7619 6428 2 (pbk)

Library of Congress catalog card record available

Typeset by Photoprint, Torquay
Printed and bound in Great Britain by Biddles Ltd, Guildford, Surrey

Contents

Introduction

Pick up and read any qualitative research article in the domain of management and organization studies, and the chances are very high that you will find a citation to Glaser and Strauss (1967). Their work, *The Discovery of Grounded Theory*, is a familiar landmark to most organization scholars who perform and/or who read qualitative studies. Perhaps because the book is widely cited, it is through the idea of grounded theory that many quantitatively trained researchers gain their introduction to qualitative methods. But, why should there be a book about it?

First, during graduate school, exposure to the procedural details of grounded theory is limited. While formal coursework in qualitative methods is increasingly appearing in Ph.D. programs in organization and management, it is still the case that many graduate students do not have access to training in qualitative methods and to focused coursework on the grounded theory approach. Similarly, compared with quantitative approaches, there are few faculty members in departments of organization and management who have pursued qualitative research in general and the grounded theory style in particular. There are also few qualitative management and organization scholars (myself included) who have been exposed to either of the originators, Barney Glaser or Anselm Strauss, or to any of their students, as a research mentor. This means that, although grounded theory as a qualitative research approach is quite visible in organization and management studies, there are limited opportunities during graduate training for in depth exploration of its research logic and procedures.

Second, citing practices indicate that organization and management scholars may not be aware of the full scope of grounded theory resources available to them. For example, methodological discussions of the grounded theory approach by the originators have appeared intermittently over a more than 30-year time period, yet, as I have pointed out elsewhere (Locke, 1997), the original 1967 monograph is often the only methodological reference to appear. In a more recent twist, Strauss and Corbin's (1990, 1998) more formulaic account is appearing as the single methodological reference to grounded theory. Other works by the originators do not seem to be considered. Related to this, resources for conducting grounded theory are spread across a number of domains, for example, sociology, nursing, education and psychology, making it difficult for organization and management scholars to track them down.

Third, as approaches and ideas are taken from one domain and put to use in another, they undergo transformation; this has been the case with grounded theory. As I shall discuss in the book, it appears that many management and organization researchers have selectively taken up grounded theory's logic and procedures, adapting and integrating them with the logic and practices from other qualitative analytic styles. To a degree, its informing logic and operational practices appear to have fractured as they have been adapted to the purposes and constraints of specific research situations and have been blended with other procedures. Certainly, the school of thought, namely symbolic interactionism, that informed the understanding of social reality expressed in grounded theory's research practices, appears to have been left behind.

In summary, even though the grounded theory approach to qualitative research is apparent through its being widely cited, the scope of work that comprises the relevant body of methodological work is, in large part, invisible. My impetus for writing this book is to restore and reveal more fully the grounded theory approach in organization and management studies. I imagine you, the readers, as graduate students and others who are interested in conducting qualitative studies of organizational and managerial life and who want to learn more about the grounded theory style of qualitative research. The creative theory building purposes of the approach are broadly appealing to many researchers whose introduction to research methods in professional schools (and the business school is certainly in that category) has strongly emphasized a logico-deductive approach executed through quantitative analytic tools. I expect that this book will be useful to those of you interested in exploring this dimension of research but who have had little exposure to grounded theory, except as a citation in publications. It will also be useful to those of you who perhaps have read one or two methodological discussions of it but have not explored the approach further. More seasoned researchers who are also interested in grounded theory but who have had little exposure to qualitative research approaches in general or this research style in particular will also find it useful.

This book, then, attempts to restore the grounded theory style of qualitative research, especially in and for scholars of organizations and management. I have borrowed the idea of restoration from Susan Leigh Star (1991), a student of one of the originators, Anselm Strauss. She characterizes the central theme in Strauss's scholarship as making visible all the work that goes into maintaining the realities of work and life that we take for granted. For the purposes of this book, restoring is interpreted in two ways. First, it involves detailing the disciplinary school of thought and procedural details of the grounded theory approach as they have been articulated by the originators, their students, and by scholars in other disciplines, including organization and management studies over the past 30 years. Second, it involves describing and discussing the use of grounded theory in studies of organization and management over the same time period. By pulling together in one place the broadly dispersed discussions of grounded theory's logic and practices in sociology, in nursing research, in education, in psychology, and also in organization and management studies, I hope to restore and reveal more fully much of the work that has gone into articulating this qualitative approach. I also hope to more fully disclose the analytic and personal work that building grounded theory requires. Similarly, by describing grounded theory in organization and management studies, including the phenomena that have been investigated, the translations of the approach's logic and procedures, and the written products that constitute grounded theories, I hope to more fully reveal the possibilities and challenges of the approach for this domain.

Organization of chapters

This book is organized into three parts. Part One of the book aims to reveal several important features of the context for the grounded theory style of qualitative research. One way to distinguish qualitative researchers is by their interest in context. We believe that it is impossible to comprehend fully a phenomenon without understanding the context in which it is expressed. Chapter 1 begins by describing the historical development of qualitative research; it explains the various paradigms of inquiry in which qualitative researchers work, locating the grounded theory approach within them. It concludes by describing other styles of qualitative research that are popular with organization and management researchers with which grounded theory co-exists. Chapter 2 continues the focus on context, taking a more disciplinary point of view. It introduces American pragmatism and the symbolic interactionist school of thought that inform this approach; it describes the sociological context in which grounded theory was articulated, and it reveals a little of the personal biographies of its originating authors. From this, I hope that readers will be able gain a sense of the history and domain of qualitative research in general (and of the organization and management area in particular), appreciating grounded theory's place in it. Further, I hope that they gain understanding of the relationship between the character of the grounded theory style of research and the features of time and its disciplinary context.

Part Two is concerned with the research approach itself. Before explicating the operational details of the approach, Chapter 3 first outlines some of its distinguishing features and clarifies the kinds of theoretical outcome grounded theory building is intended to achieve. It also introduces readers to the language terms used to speak about such theories. Chapter 4 focuses on the research logic and basic operational procedures as they were initially articulated. It details the processes through which meaning is assigned to qualitative data and data sampling is executed. It also provides some of the criteria by which grounded theories are evaluated. Chapter 5 brings Part Two to a close by delineating procedural developments in grounded theory analysis that have followed during the last 30 years (including divergence in these developments on the part of the originators), and by considering some of the personal tensions researchers face when they execute this research approach. I hope that readers will take away from this section a basic understanding of the procedures of grounded theory. Of course, while important, this understanding is nothing without researcher experience. Researchers will have to embark on their own grounded theory studies, breathing life into the words through which the procedures are described with the details of their own experience. I also hope that readers will seek out and draw on the many methodological discussions referenced, deepening their understanding of the approach.

Part Three moves more fully into revealing grounded theory in the domain of organization and management studies, examining how it has traveled and been translated as it has been adopted and adapted here. The particular features of grounded theory building that make it suitable for studies in our domain are suggested in Chapter 6. It also describes and demonstrates how grounded theory has been adopted, and it details the ways in which management researchers have adapted it, integrating new procedures and orienting schools of thought into the approach. The kinds of theory organization and management researchers have developed are illustrated, and Chapter 6 closes by considering possible constraints that the study of corporate organizations and management might impose on grounded theory procedures. Chapter 7 examines grounded theory in studies of organization and management as a composed research product. Here the book pays particular attention to the crafting of a grounded theory journal article. It describes the character of grounded theories in management and organization studies and examines how they are textually presented. I hope that readers will take from Part Three a sense of the challenges and opportunities associated with using this style of research, and that they will be inspired by the breadth and variety of published work that has drawn on it.

A note on the perspective of the author

Before concluding this introduction, a final note on the perspective I bring to this project and to methodological accounts in general. I began qualitative studies as an undergraduate when working with a group of ethologists. I learned to make systematic and detailed observations that were then converted into frequency data – very much in the tradition of more modernist content analysis practiced today. I came later in graduate work to the issue of meaning and interpretation, and have since adopted an interpretive perspective in my work. With the focus this perspective provides on how realities are constructed, I am aware of the constructed character of methodological accounts. Descriptions of particular methods of research obviously take place as retrospective accounts. They are reports written after the bulk of research practices have been concluded, rather than being narrated moment by moment within the stream of acts that comprise the research method in-use (Vidich and Lyman, 1994, p. 24). As such, they condense what was originally experienced into a set of coherent images that often omit much of the *ad hoc*, opportunistic, and problem solving nature of the inquiry process. Knorr-Cetina's work (1981) that provides a description of how research chemists, for example, fashion a textually linear account out of a nonlinear research process as they prepare their work for formal publication highlights this. Specifically, it brings out the discrepancies between the coherence articulated in representations of research processes and the disjointedness of research as an act in progress.

Furthermore, the disembodied, general and technical language displayed by such texts conforms very closely to the rhetoric traditionally associated with all 'scientific writing' (Golden-Biddle and Locke, 1997; Selzer, 1993). The language and the research processes they describe easily take on the form of textbook ideals (Vidich and Lyman, 1994).

I have made some deliberate choices in writing this book to highlight the constructed character of our research efforts. The decision to devote a whole part of the book to grounded theory's historical, disciplinary context and to include the biographies of the originators was made *not* to write the procedures as disembodied, impersonal, and a-historical, but to place them in a time, location, and in particular 'bodies.' I have also made some deliberate choices in the language that I use to describe the research process. Specifically, when talking about analysis, I have chosen to use wording that highlights the agency of researchers who actively compose their analytic categories and research findings. This contrasts with the language of the originators, so prevalent at the time in which they wrote their monograph, which suggests a more passive role in which some external reality might be 'discovered' by application of the appropriate procedures. And, I have chosen to reveal my own agency in writing this text.

Part One

Situating the Discovery of Grounded Theory

1

Situating the discovery of grounded theory within the tradition of qualitative methods

In 1967 Barney Glaser and Anselm Strauss published *The Discovery of Grounded Theory*. It was their formal description of the approach to handling and interpreting qualitative data that they had developed in the early 1960s during what is described as a participant observation study of hospital staff's care and management of dying patients. As originally stated, they characterize this research approach as one oriented towards the inductive generation of theory from data that has been systematically obtained and analyzed (Glaser and Strauss, 1967). Some 30+ years have passed since the publication of that monograph. During this time, the general approach to qualitative data analysis and theory development articulated in that volume has both persisted and been taken up in disciplines outside its originating domain of sociology. The grounded theory style of qualitative research has traveled extensively, for example, to psychology, to information science, to education, to many communities of practice within health care, and, of course, to management and organization studies. Indeed, in the domain of qualitative research, the original text has assumed canonical status. Norman Denzin, one of the editors of the widely read and cited *Handbook of Qualitative Research*, underscores the status of this approach to qualitative research with the startling statement that 'the grounded theory perspective is the most widely used qualitative interpretive framework in the social sciences today' (1994: 508). He takes his point even further, noting that 'when one peels back the layers of discourse embedded in any of the numerous qualitative guides to interpretation and theory construction, the core features of the Strauss approach are present, even when Strauss and associates are not directly named' (1994: 513).

Interestingly, despite the visibility and status of the *Discovery* book, at this point in time, just what constitutes grounded theory is by no means an unequivocal or an uncontested issue. As I shall discuss in more detail a little later, grounded theory has evolved and adapted as its research practices have been further articulated and extended by its originators, their students, and other methodologists who have taken up this style of inquiry. In addition, those substantive researchers who have found its guidance useful and who have adapted and incorporated it into their own work have further interpreted its research practices. By the late 1980s and early 1990s, the nature of grounded theorizing became an issue, and it was being explicitly contested by the originators of the approach and their respective students (Glaser, 1992; Locke, 1997; Stern, 1994; Strauss and Corbin, 1990).

What I should like to do in Part One of this book, by way of an introduction to the analytic research practices and conceptual products indicated by the term 'grounded theory,' is to provide some background and context for this research approach before moving on, in Part Two, to outline the research process as it was initially articulated. It makes sense to begin, I think, with the perspective afforded by a number of different but interrelated histories. These are: the research tradition that falls under the rubric of qualitative methods; the disciplinary domain of sociology, particularly the symbolic interactionist tradition and its informing American pragmatist philosophy; and, of course, the personal biographies of the original monograph's authors. For, as Denzin & Lincoln (1994) suggest, behind any work stand the personal biographies of culturally and historically situated researchers. Typically, grounded theory's 'origination story' represents it as being developed and articulated within the context of a particular research program on dying in medical institutions that was carried out in northern California over a six-year period in the late 1950s and early 1960s. However, this research approach is also a product of the authors' location within a community of research practice, a particular disciplinary tradition, and, of course, their particular biographies within both at a particular moment in time. All three histories guided and shaped *The Discovery of Grounded Theory*.

These discussions will provide a foundation for understanding the character of grounded theory both as a research process and as a particular research product. Of course, the stories of contexts and histories that follow are similarly situated ones, and they express a coherence that I am composing in grounded theory's intellectual tradition, its research practices and the personal biographies of its originators. Here in Chapter 1, I sketch the domain of qualitative research and grounded theory's place in it by first providing one perspective on qualitative research's development over the last 90 years. In doing this, I underscore the methodological issues that absorbed researcher attention during the various stages of its history. The chapter then considers the different research paradigms in which these same issues find current expression in the qualitative study of organization and management. This introduction to the domain of qualitative research closes by reviewing several other styles of qualitative research practice with which grounded theory co-exists.

A historical perspective on the practice of qualitative methods

Moments in the development of qualitative research
The beginning of qualitative research methods as professionally established practices for generating knowledge in the human disciplines is often located in the early 1900s within two social science domains: sociology, with the 'Chicago School's' qualitative approach to the study of group life, and anthropology, with the tradition of fieldwork established by such notables as Bateson, Boaz, Evans-Pritchard, Radcliffe-Brown and Malinowski (Denzin and Lincoln, 1994). (I should note that this representation of these disciplines as discrete is somewhat misleading, because up until the 1950s they were often practiced within the same University department under one administrator (Van Maanen, 1988)). In these disciplines at this time, modern social science researchers were concerned with producing valid and objective interpretations of social groups studied through field based qualitative procedures.

In the 90 or so years since those beginnings, Denzin and Lincoln (1994) outline what they term five moments of qualitative research practice. These moments are: the traditional, the modernist, the moment of blurred genres, the crisis of representation, and the double crisis. Each of these moments represents a period of time in which a discernible set of issues and considerations became evident in the field of qualitative research. The issues and considerations that arose in them highlight different perspectives on knowledge, the role of the researcher in making it, and the language through which such knowledge is presented. Consequently they affected the way that researchers within the qualitative tradition practiced, understood, reflected on, and wrote about their craft. Although each of these moments is associated with a particular point of time during the recent 90 years, the view of research practice expressed in each of them persists and still operates into the present. The result is that qualitative research today is a practice domain populated by many viewpoints and styles of practice.

Denzin and Lincoln (1994) identify that first moment when fieldwork became professionally established in sociology and anthropology as the 'traditional' moment. In sociology (in the United States, at least), this moment is often marked by the initial publication in 1918 of Thomas and Znaniecki's *The Polish Peasant in Europe and America*. This was a monumental fieldwork-based and theoretically oriented empirical effort whose composed results ran to well over two thousand pages. One of its authors, W.I. Thomas, was influential at the University of Chicago, as was Robert E. Park. Under the latter's direction, the 'Chicago School,' as it came to be called, was responsible for producing a set of ethnographic studies that focused on particularized descriptions of various aspects of human life that they perceived to be emerging in the city (Vidich and Lyman, 1994).

While qualitative sociologists, especially Chicago sociologists, were out studying life near to home, their disciplinary siblings in anthropology went abroad to conduct first hand extended field studies of 'other' races and cultures of the world and to bring back accounts of their lives. Bronislaw Malinowski's *Argonauts of the Western Pacific* (1922) is regarded by many as the quintessential anthropological ethnography of this moment. Similarly, Margaret Mead's (1928) account of life in Samoa provides a straightforward depiction of the lives of 'others' who live in distant lands. In both sociology and anthropology, the written knowledge products that resulted from these studies were taken to be real and accurate reports of the lives and worlds of their subjects. The role of researchers was as observer of the lives and worlds of the subject, and the language of their knowledge texts was viewed as providing a literal representation of those worlds.

The traditional moment was followed in the years after World War II by a second, 'modernist,' one that continued, and continues today, to embrace social realism. This modern moment celebrates researcher ability to accurately portray the social situation and subjects they study. Many management and organization scholars, particularly those with an interest in qualitative methods, will be familiar with the work of William Foote Whyte, whose accounts of Italian American life in 'Cornerville' (1955) demonstrate both their Chicago heritage and their commitment to a realist portrayal of life on the street. In this moment, the role of authors and the language through which they construct the social reality they studied continue to be taken for granted. Language is conceived as a tool that reflects discovered phenomena, and in this moment, researchers ask no questions about the agency of the researcher in producing knowledge about the social situation studied nor do they examine just what is being represented in the written products of their investigative efforts. This social realist perspective on writing and language, as Rorty (1982) points out, construes writing as an intermediary between these discovered phenomena and their portrayal in disciplinary texts such as the research monograph or journal article. In time, however, questions were raised about just what qualitative researchers had been taking for granted as they conducted their studies and composed their research products for publication.

The modernist moment was then, in its turn, followed in the 1970s and early 1980s by the moment of 'blurred genres.' In this moment, the notions of social realism and objectivist knowledge were challenged, as many qualitative researchers embraced the position that knowledge making is fundamentally an act of interpretation. It was in this moment that qualitative research took its 'interpretive turn' (Rabinow and Sullivan, 1979: 1), highlighting among other things the role played by culture and context, including those of researchers, in the interpretation of human activity. Geertz' (1973) phrase 'blurred genres' similarly echoes interpretivism through the idea that distinctions between the social sciences and the humanities were no longer tenable. Consistent with this idea, questions were raised about the privileged status accorded to researchers' accounts of the situations they studied. From the vantage of this moment, language becomes a problematic issue; its ability to reflect reality is actively considered and challenged. Accordingly, research accounts are conceived as fundamentally interpretive rather than objective.

During the mid-1980s, this interpretive turn developed more fully. At this time, scholars directly challenged our modernist assumptions that there are 'real' social realities, subjects, and theories that can be veridic-ally expressed through language (Cunliffe, 2000). Rather, language is understood to be a medium that can create only a particular view of reality. It takes on particular significance as the site where social realities are created because language defines both what we know about a situation and how we know it – it produces the very objects of which it speaks (Hardy and Palmer, 1999). Objectivity and its correspondence to reality were thus disputed, and the status of language shifted from being literal to being seen as metaphorical and constitutive of 'reality' (Cunliffe, 2000). This led to a re-examination of the role of researchers, the language of knowledge bearing texts, and to a concern with 'reflex-ivity.' The latter underscores the importance of reflecting on assumptions that we as researchers make when we produce what we regard as knowledge (Cunliffe, 2000; Hardy and Palmer, 1999).

Not surprisingly, from the vantage of this moment, the knowledge texts produced during earlier periods were viewed quite differently. For example, the work of the traditional and modernist moments was reconceived. While the knowledge texts of classical anthropologists like the ones mentioned continued to be studied for the stories they told about conducting and writing fieldwork (e.g. Wax, 1972), their repre-sentation of social worlds and subjects were strongly criticized for constituting them according to a colonial ethos (Rosaldo, 1989). Geertz (1988) drew attention to the authorial styles of particular anthropologists, underscoring how they portrayed those they studied. Within manage-ment and organization studies, Van Maanen (1988) explored 'realist' ethnographic tales for the ways in which their language constructs those 'real' realities of other people and worlds. While 'realist' texts were critiqued, researchers probed the possibility of more reflexive writing. In some of these explorations, researchers attempt to disclose their agency by writing themselves into their knowledge texts (Van Maanen, 1988). In others, researchers set aside the traditional form of the scientific research monograph and experimented with a wide range of narrative forms and devices (see Ellis and Bochner, 1996; Richardson, 1995). A provocative example of writing knowledge differently is Marianne Paget's (1995) production of a performance text; yes, she performed the work.

The present fifth moment of 'double crisis' is characterized as a poststructural or postmodern one. The double crisis continues the previous moment's focus on representation, but it takes the concerns with representation further, challenging the possibility of ever establishing the realities of lived experience in the social scene studied or the identity and values of the researcher apart from the language through which both are represented. The moment of 'double crises' raises the possibility that knowledge can never be established or settled in any ultimate sense. From the vantage of this unsettling moment, there is no such thing as reality; reality is an image created by the language we use. Furthermore, there are multiple versions of such reality, none of which is more or less real than the other, though some versions are more privileged than others (Hardy and Palmer, 1999). During this moment, researchers increasingly became interested in the political dimensions of texts. The latter were viewed as mechanisms for creating and maintaining particular relations of power that gave voice to some while excluding others, and researchers understood their role as taking on the voice of those silenced others. During this moment, critical and feminist research approaches took hold.

While the issues and concerns recognized in each of these moments were initially articulated outside management and organization studies in domains such as anthropology, sociology and cultural studies, they of course have been taken up by qualitative researchers in management. Each of these moments finds expression in our own discipline where it is now commonplace to conceive and speak of qualitative research as falling within one of three paradigms: modern, interpretive and postmodern (Hatch, 1997). Guba and Lincoln (1994) build on Thomas Kuhn's (1970) ideas about paradigms as constellations of values, beliefs and methodological assumptions embedded in particular views of the world to compose the following definition. A paradigm is a set of basic beliefs about the nature of reality, the nature of the relationship between researchers and the worlds and subjects they study, and the methods through which knowledge can be achieved. As Guba and Lincoln point out, these 'beliefs are basic in the sense that they must be accepted simply on faith (however well argued); there is no way to establish their ultimate truthfulness' (1994: 107).

Roughly speaking, the second modernist moment corresponds to the realist stance of the modernist paradigm; the third and fourth moments are incorporated within the interpretive paradigm; and the fifth moment of double crisis is consistent with postmodernism . Qualitative research is practiced by management and organization scholars from each of these paradigms across a number of communities of research practice. Let us briefly touch on these paradigms as well on some of the variety expressed in qualitative research practice.

Qualitative research paradigms in studies of management and organization

The modernist paradigm

The modernist paradigm continues the grand project begun around the time of Descartes to displace a dependency on faith as the source of knowledge with a reliance on reason. The modernist emphasis is on explanations of how the world works that ultimately could be harnessed towards its prediction and control. Accordingly, inquiry is directed towards the discovery of empirical facts and universal laws of cause and effect that are to be embedded in an explanatory or theoretical framework. Such abstract theoretical frameworks would clarify and integrate the facts and the laws that govern the way the world works, and would hold independent of time and context (Guba and Lincoln, 1994).

Modernism assumes a realist ontology. It supposes that an objective world exists as a knowable observable reality and that the facts of and laws governing that world are given and independent of those who might observe them. This world is investigated primarily through a hypothetico-deductive method in which prior theory plays a primary role (Bryman, 1988). First, hypotheses about the way the world likely works are advanced; then they are tested against that world. In practice, this means that research in the modernist tradition is directed towards elaborating theories whose approximations to reality are composed in the form of *a priori* hypotheses that are verified or refuted against the referent of observed reality (Denzin and Lincoln, 1994). Knowledge consequently takes the form of substantiated propositions that can be accepted as facts or laws because they have been checked against reality. This perspective is illustrated in Ross and Staw's (1993) qualitative case study of the Shoreham nuclear power plant. In this study, Ross and Staw 'tested' a four-stage temporal model of organizational escalation that had been derived from prior work. In their words, the study of Shoreham was designed to provide an 'independent test of Propositions 1 and 2' – elements of their temporal model of organizational escalation (1993: 703).

The modernist stance is also evident in the style of qualitative data analysis termed 'content analysis.' Some time ago, as an undergraduate in the psychology department of University College London, I rejected the instruction I had received in experimental design that had been my research preparation for an honors thesis in favor of a more direct and natural approach to research. (Obviously, my own commitments to research style surfaced quite early). Signing up with the small band of ethologists who occupied a corner of the department, my first qualitative project involved operational practices that are at the heart of content analysis. These are: detailed observations of social activity gathered via field work; the creation of conceptual categories; and the development of frequency counts of the occurrence of the conceptual categories in the field observations that enabled the quantitative testing of propositions.

Closer to the domain of management and organization studies, Richard Boyatsis drew on these practices in a study designed to determine which managerial characteristics were related to effective performance (1982). In one phase of the study, transcripts were developed from interviews during which respondents were asked to describe incidents of on-the-job effectiveness and ineffectiveness. A coding system was developed to analyze these interview based observations. Previous work provided the basis from which 19 conceptual categories that comprised this study's coding system were developed. The interview transcripts were independently coded by two coders for frequency of occurrence of each of the 19 categories. The frequencies determined for the conceptual categories then formed the basis for making comparisons of managers in high, average, and low performance groupings. The resulting correlations pointed to those characteristics that distinguished high from low performance.

As this brief illustration indicates, modernist qualitative researchers share with quantitative investigators a concern for the nature of the relationship between their discovered facts and the observable world that these purport to explain. Specifically, in order for these facts and relationships to earn their way into a broad theoretical framework, they must meet a number of criteria. Their appropriateness for inclusion is evaluated by the extent to which the researcher's findings accurately map the aspect of the social world studied (internal validity); the extent to which the findings hold for other social settings and actors that are similar to the one studied (generalizability); the extent to which the findings persist and are able to be reproduced (reliability); and the extent to which the findings are independent of and free from any bias (Guba and Lincoln, 1994).

In terms of qualitative research, these criteria are evident in a number of research practices. Given that qualitative researchers often focus on few cases, and therefore small sample sizes, they have generally made strong claims for the internal validity of their findings. Further, the issue of potential bias is often addressed through the use of multiple coders whose individual application of the codes can be compared. For example, Fox-Wolfgramm (1997) emphasizes the importance of achieving interrater reliability in analyses of qualitative data.

The interpretive paradigm

The interpretive (and related constructivist) paradigms are distinguished by an interest in understanding the world of lived experience from the point of view of those who live it. Their concern, therefore, is with a subjective reality. Researchers working in this paradigm focus on particular situated actors who they construe as composing meaning out of events and phenomena through prolonged processes of interaction that involve history, language and action. Thus, social reality is not a given. It is built up over time through shared history, experience and communication so that what is taken for 'reality' is what is shared and taken for granted as to the way the world is to be perceived and understood. Interpretive social research, then, focuses on what events and objects mean to people, on how they perceive what happens to them and around them, and on how they adapt their behavior in light of these meanings and perspectives (Rubin and Rubin, 1995). Because meaning is composed through situated interaction, the interpretive approach makes the assumption that meaning is not standardized from place to place or person to person. Interpretive researchers accept that values and views may well differ across groups and across social settings, and they appreciate that shared meaning is an achievement.

Interpretivists believe that in order to understand this world, researchers must engage with and participate in it, and they must actively interpret it. That is, to prepare an interpretation researchers must first participate in the social world in order to better understand it before they compose and offer their construction of the meaning systems of the social actors they study (Schwandt, 1994). Interpretive researchers, therefore, use methods like participant observation and ethnographic interviewing to try to elicit organization members' perspectives on the social worlds they live in, their work, and the events they observed or were party to.

This tradition obviously has an understanding of method that is inconsistent with the modernist concern with discovering universally applicable laws or structuring principals to explain behavior and with the elimination of personal subjective judgment expressed in notions such as verification and testability. Rather than method being a tool that when followed eliminates human judgment, interpretivism conceives of method as a tool to assist judgment. Of course, there is a certain tension between the interpretivist's interest in the first-hand subjective experience of those they study and their equal interest in constructing an external, even objectified, account of that experience (Denzin, 1992). Researchers in this paradigm aim to make responsible interpretations and to provide solid bases for them. However, interpretivism takes for granted that researcher agency in formulating judgments cannot be eliminated, because social scientists are caught in the same human meaning making web as those that they study (Rabinow and Sullivan, 1979). Researchers consequently attempt to be 'up front' with their readers and 'confess' (Van Maanen, 1988) their values and interests.

Most organization scholars likely associate *The Social Construction of Reality* (Berger and Luckmann, 1967), written by sociologists, with this paradigm. Within organization studies, Hatch (1997) has argued that this interpretive tradition is expressed in Karl Weick's (1969) enactment theory, which underscores the active role that organization members play in creating the very organizations in which they work. Hatch (1997) suggests an interpretive view is expressed in two ways: first, in recognizing the constitutive nature of language so that by using ideas like organization we actively create it as phenomena; and second, by highlighting that what organizational actors take as being real is subjective. Other examples of interpretive work include: Gephart's (1978) study of organization succession that focuses on the language and activities through which succession is created; Isabella's (1990) study of middle managers in a financial services institution, underscoring that changes in managers' understanding and interpretations of organizational events are necessary in order for a change process to advance; Bartunek's (1984) study of a religious order that explores the relationship between organization members' interpretive schemes and organization structure; and Cunliffe's (in press) exploration of how managers act as practical authors of present and possible future organizational realities through their conversations. All of these studies highlight the way in which meaning making or interpretive activities construct and shape organizational and management realities.

The postmodern paradigm
The term postmodern was initially popularized in the arts, literary criticism and philosophy. Parker (1992) suggests that postmodernism was expressed in the architectural profession in proposals that architectural design eschew monolithic modern structures in favor of design that displayed characteristics that challenged such convention. Designs which took traditional concepts of buildings and reinterpreted them, for example, by laying them on their sides, or turning them upside down, or fracturing them, or . . . were to be encouraged. Best and Kellner (1997) take the 'radical intellectuals of the 1960s' (for example, Michel Foucault, Jacques Derrida, Jean-Francois Lyotard, and Jean Baudrillard) as the first postmodern theorists, linking their ideas to the social upheaval taking place in France and the United States during the 1960s. Best and Kellner (1997) suggest that experiences of such social upheaval, for example, protests against the Vietnam war in the United States and the protests in France when students and workers occupied universities and factories, forcing then President de Gaulle to flee 'to come up with a solution', produced an openness to notions of discontinuity and rupture.

Today, a huge variety of ideas are submitted to the label 'postmodern' and, to touch on what will be a recurrent theme, it is not one school. As the previous discussion of the moment of double crisis indicated, though, a recurrent interest in postmodern work is in examining how power relations privilege particular world views while silencing others. The question of 'truth' is to be answered by disclosing which or whose truth is true! Not surprisingly, one dimension of postmodern thinking focuses on the problematic nature of scientific activity. Here, post-modernism argues for a basic rejection of the notion that science can be viewed as objective or value free because the assumptions underlying scientific activity and the projects in which scientists engage are always set by the wider culture, politics, values, and historical period in which they are embedded. Science is, therefore, understood to be a practical accomplishment achieved by scientists as a community (Hassard, 1990).

Postmodernism directly challenges the modernist research aim of achieving general, integrated, explanatory and predictive frameworks with its own view of knowledge as fundamentally fragmented and unstable. Furthermore, expectations that what is understood as know-ledge can be integrated into a unified whole are not only questionable, they are also viewed as a kind of intellectual imperialism that ignores the fundamental instability of 'reality' (Hatch, 1997; Parker, 1992). Post-modernism suggests that what is taken for 'reality' is constructed by the discursive or language systems put in play by a particular social histor-ical context – what is 'real' then is what is represented as such. And, researchers' own attempts at uncovering 'reality' should also be seen as forms of discourse (Parker, 1992). Indeed, postmodern theory has as one of its aims the deconstruction of grand narratives of truth and know-ledge (Kincheloe and McLaren, 1994). Accordingly, a discernible focus of postmodern research attention has been the scientific 'authoritative' text, and, more specifically, researchers have attended to the way in which 'truth effects' are achieved via textual strategies (Linstead, 1993).

With this highly problematic notion of discourse, not surprisingly postmodernists focus attention on power interests – whose voices have a place and whose voices are excluded – in current knowledge making practices. For many postmodern investigators, therefore, research is a political act and diversity and pluralism are central themes in their work. Research activity in this paradigm frequently draws on literary criticism and especially on the close deconstructive reading advanced by Derrida (1978) to investigate the textual construction of 'truth' and 'reality.' Examples of such work in management and organization studies include: Calas and Smircich's (1990) work, which examines organizational theorizing on leadership, drawing on feminist deconstructive strategies to highlight the cultural influences and constraints on this 'knowledge;' Martin's (1990) explication of gender conflict in an organization's response to the maternity leave of one of its female officers; Boje's (1995) account of the multiple and suppressed realities that constituted Disney; and Covaleski et al.'s (1998) use of Foucault's ideas about power and knowledge to describe how mentoring and management by objectives serve as techniques of control. In these works, the notions of multiple, disparate realities, power, and suppressed voices are thematic.

From the perspective of each of these three paradigms, Hatch (1997) indicates that organization studies can take on quite different meanings and methods. From the standpoint of modernism, organization studies would be the investigation of objective realities to be explained and controlled through the application of impartial rational and precise methods, hence the favoring of mathematically informed methods. From the interpretive vantage, management and organization studies would involve the study of those symbolic processes through which subjective experiences of organization are created; such a study is best achieved through methods like participant observation and ethnographic interviewing that take the researcher close to the experiences of those she studies. And, from the perspective of postmodernism, organization studies would take as their subject organization theory and the theorizing practices of their scholars as well as the organizational theories and ideologies of actors. Consequently, methods imported from literary theory, such as deconstruction and criticism, are favored as well as the critical approaches of Marxism and feminist theory (Hatch, 1997).

Locating grounded theory in moments and paradigms

What then of grounded theory? In which historical moment did it appear and within what paradigm is it situated? In their historically oriented framework, Lincoln and Denzin place *The Discovery of Grounded Theory* in the second modernist phase of qualitative research. Indeed, they identify it as one of several monographs that attempted to bring more formalization and systematization to qualitative methods during the post war years (Denzin and Lincoln, 1994). Certainly, there is much in the original monograph that expresses the realist concerns of the modernist time period in which it was written and that invites readers to locate the research approach with the modernist research paradigm. Indicators of a modernist perspective are carried forward into the originator's subsequent methodological texts. For example, the recurrent use of language terms such as 'emergence' and 'discovery' and theory grounded in 'reality' in the original monograph are strongly suggestive of an objective realist perspective. And, in this decade, there is an expressed concern with such modernist criteria as verifying hypotheses, the replicability of findings, and researcher bias (Corbin and Strauss, 1990; Strauss and Corbin, 1994).

On the other hand, grounded theory's concern with subjective experience stemming, as we shall shortly discuss, from its heritage in American pragmatism and the symbolic interactionist school of sociology, suggests that the grounded theory approach might be more appropriately located within the interpretive paradigm (Lowenberg, 1993). Over the years, the concerns articulated in the interpretive moment do enter into the originators' methodological discussions, and many claims do take on the language associated with interpretivism. For example, Strauss and Corbin (1994: 280) state that 'grounded theory requires that the interpretations and perspectives of actors on their own and others' actions become incorporated into our own [meaning researcher] interpretations.' Interestingly, Strauss (1987) had commented that as regards the disparate perspectives of knowledge as science, as compared with a view of knowledge in more humanistic terms, his position lay somewhere between.

Clearly, the paradigm lines are not always clearly drawn. When they are, they are determined more by the commitments of individual researchers than by the operational practices of a research approach. Thus, the grounded theory style has subsequently been used by Glaser and Strauss' students and others in more wholly interpretive studies (e.g. Charmaz, 1990) and also in feminist theorizing (Henwood and Pidgeon, 1995; Keddy et al., 1996). In management and organization studies, the approach has been invoked in works that are modernist in their orientation (e.g. Eisenhardt, 1989a; Kram and Isabella, 1985; Rafaeli and Sutton, 1991; Ross and Staw, 1993), in works that fall within the interpretive paradigm (Gephart, 1993; Gioia and Chittipeddi, 1991; Locke and Golden-Biddle, 1997; Prasad, 1993; Turner, 1976), and also in postmodern approaches (Covaleski et al., 1998).

Management and organization's diverse communities of qualitative research practice

The different paradigms just discussed do not account for all of the diversity in qualitative research within management and organization studies. Besides working from different research paradigms, qualitative investigators also work in various approaches or styles that reflect their orientation to particular communities of research practice. Three such communities that are significantly represented among qualitative researchers are ethnography, action research and case work. Before moving on to outline their distinguishing characteristics, a word of caution is perhaps in order. Drawing distinctions and boundaries between one area of inquiry and another is always slippery work because it requires a reduction and simplification of the research style of different communities of research practitioners. Within those particular communities, whether they are 'action researchers,' 'case researchers,' 'ethnographers,' or 'grounded theory researchers,' individuals may have as much that is different about their particular research practices as they have in common. Indeed, within each of the communities of practice that I shall touch on below, there are schools of thought and practice that represent modern, interpretive, and postmodern interpretations of the research act and its resultant research products.

Similarly, across different research practice communities, researchers may share much in terms of their general methodological procedures. Indeed, the particular constraints created by all qualitative work, such as the need to collect a data set, to fracture it for manipulation, somehow to label and reorder the fractured elements, and so on, mean that the overall shape of qualitative data analysis will be quite similar (Turner, 1988) regardless of the community with which qualitative researchers may identify.

Consequently, it is with this in mind that I wearily consider the distinguishing characteristics of other approaches or styles that fall under the umbrella of qualitative research and that are widely used within the domain of organization studies.

Action research

Action research in America is largely associated with the work of Kurt Lewin, who was interested in directing scientific approaches to improving the major social problems of the times, such as racism and social unrest (Lewin, 1951). Lewin insisted that combining 'action' and 'research' was methodologically sound, arguing that an understanding of a social system could best be achieved by first introducing change into it and then observing its effects. At about the same time in the United Kingdom (shortly after World War II), there was a move towards this form of research by a group of scholars who later were to form the Tavistock Institute for Human Relations (Elden and Chisolm, 1993). The action research practice community is generally distinguished by two commitments: a commitment to learning by attempting to bring about some form of organizational transformation and a commitment to involving in the research and change process those organizational members likely to be affected. Consequently, action researchers attend to executing research processes that are relevant both for scholars interested in creating knowledge and for practitioners struggling with particular sets of problems (Baburoglu and Ravn, 1992). It distinguishes itself as a methodological approach in its dual purposes of providing practical advice and advancing knowledge.

To achieve this, action researchers deliberately aim to contribute to two domains. In the organizational community in which they are temporarily involved, action researchers actively participate in the very phenomenon they are studying in order to develop the organizational competencies of individual organizational actors (Susman and Evered, 1978), to develop the learning capacities of the organization as a whole (Argyris and Shon, 1978), and thereby to influence the course of events (Gummesson, 1991). In the professional scholarly community in which they are ongoing members, they intend to advance understanding of the change process and of the possibilities for organization.

As a research approach, action research is generally conceived as a cyclical and multi-phased inquiry process. It begins with problem diagnosis, progresses to the planning and design of action steps, carries forward with their implementation, and pauses with a subsequent evaluation of outcomes that will inform further diagnosis (Elden and Chisolm, 1993). One of the classic studies exhibiting this research approach is Coch and French's (1948) action research experiment at Harwood manufacturing, a pajama plant in Marion, Virginia. Coch and French were interested in exploring why the young women who worked in the plant resisted changes to improve operations. Their study began with a series of observations about the behavior of changed groups in order to devise a working theory that would account for the phenomenon of resistance. On the basis of their theory, which focused on resistance to change as an outcome of frustration and group induced forces, they designed and conducted a real life experiment in the factory. Their experimental manipulation focused on the effect that group participation in designing change might have on behavior. Its status as a field experiment was underscored in the creation of not only experimental but also control groups who were denied the opportunity to participate in the design of their work, and the development of a set of measures by which the outcomes of the manipulation might be gauged.

Over the years, the basic commitments of the action research community have evolved and today there are many forms of action research practice. In 1993 the journal *Human Relations* devoted a special issue to exploring varieties of action research. One form of action research that has gained increasing attention is termed 'co-operative inquiry' (Reason, 1988, 1994; Reason and Heron, 1986). Co-operative inquiry focuses largely on individual rather than organizational change, and it has its roots in humanistic psychology's contention that individuals can, with support, choose to transform how they live their lives (Reason, 1994). The extension of action research's commitment to involving organization members in the research and change process involves them as full partners in the research and change process. This form of action research aims to make change and learning a self-generating process in those systems in which action researchers engage. The action researchers' goals, therefore, are not only to deal with specific problems, but to leave their subject partners with higher levels of self-determination and self-development (Elden and Chisolm, 1993).

Case studies
Widely used within organizational studies, case studies are perhaps the most difficult research approach to distinguish at this time. For example, characterizations of case studies as a research strategy that 'focuses on dynamics present within single settings' (Eisenhardt, 1989b: 534) or that is distinguished by its 'attempts to examine a contemporary phenomenon in its real life context' (Yin, 1981: 59) overlap considerably with all other naturalistically oriented qualitative research approaches. Post and Andrews, for example, acknowledge that 'case research is often a euphemism for qualitative research' (1982: 18). Ragin (1992) confirms that despite the centrality of case studies to social scientific talk and their widespread use, case analysis is poorly defined – or, perhaps a better statement would be that it is pluralistically defined. Thus, he points out

that cases may be conceived as empirical units or as theoretical constructs – as inputs to or outcomes from the investigative process. And, Wolcott comments that when he tried to locate case studies with other styles of qualitative research, it appeared 'to fit everywhere in general and yet nowhere in particular' (1992: 36); consequently, he chose to regard case studies as a research product, a format for reporting qualitative descriptive work.

Indeed, to the extent that I dare risk a definition of the case study, I find compelling Stake's statement that 'case study is not a methodological choice, but a choice of object to be studied' (1994: 236). Case studies, therefore, are distinguished by the researcher's interest in studying particular objects – or bounded systems. According to Post and Andrews (1982), the object to be studied can be: a single or several organizations, for example, a business firm; one or more organizational sub-units, for instance, strategic business units; a particular organizational practice like strategic decision making; and one or more industries where the research might focus on competitors and producers of substitute goods or services. In studies of organization and management, investigations that describe themselves as case studies, generally focus on macro, organizational or industry levels of analysis. Most organization theorists would agree that Lawrence and Lorsch's (1967) study of organization and environment is a 'classic' in case study research within this domain.

Stake (1994, 1995) describes three types of case study. The first type, the intrinsic case study, focuses on the uniqueness of a particular case; analysts are interested simply in understanding the case itself – this particular organization – for all its particularity and uniqueness. By contrast, in the second type of case study, instrumental cases, researchers are interested in a particular case because of the potential it has to offer in providing insight into a substantive issue or to advance theory. When instrumental case studies extend into the study of more than one case, they become collective studies. The Lawrence and Lorsch (1967) study was of this type. They studied 10 organizations within a single industry (Lawrence, 1981). This third form of case study is more recently in Yin's (1994) approach to case study research, an approach now favored by several organization researchers working in the modern paradigm. Accordingly, Yin's approach assumes that researchers can objectively establish the facts of a particular case, that research ought to be theory-driven, and that multiple case studies should be designed around the kind of 'replication' logic found in the design of scientific experiments (Yin, 1998).

Regardless of the type of case study, the case approach does not favor any particular type of information – qualitative or quantitative. For example, the well-known Aston Studies included quantitative as well as qualitative data. Researchers in this program employed many measures that varied in type, sophistication and complexity to examine organizational structure and context (Pugh, 1988). Similarly, in the study of organization and environment, Lawrence and Lorsch's data derived from interviews with senior executives, a number of questionnaire based instruments and various economic indicators (Lawrence, 1981).

In terms of analytic strategies, case studies do seem to share the practice of producing a first-order, factually based descriptive account (Van Maanen, 1979) – the case – of the units that are studied. Frequently, some form of analysis is then applied to those accounts (e.g. Brown and Eisenhardt, 1997). The procedures through which the gathered interview, observational, and quantitative data are reduced to fashion such accounts, however, are not always clear and do not seem to be codified.

To the extent that case studies are distinguished by the researcher's choice of an investigative object – issues of sampling are of central concern. Lawrence (1981) explains that the particular 10 organizations were selected for the organization and environment study in order to maximize differences in business environment and economic performance for the organizations. The can industry was selected because of its stability. Choice of the case or cases for study, in this and other case study researches, reflects purposeful sampling – that is the selection of cases that provide the opportunity to learn a great deal about issues central to the research (Patton, 1990). Patton (1990) offers some 15 different strategies to help the researcher think about the process of purposefully selecting information rich cases; some of these include sampling of deviant cases, sampling for maximum variation, and sampling for a specific criterion. Similarly, others suggest that selection may focus on a single site or a collection of sites; it may involve multiple settings within a site selection; it may be focused on a particular issue; it may focus on the ordinary or typical, or it may focus on the unusual (Stake, 1995; Yin, 1994).

Ethnography

Modern ethnography is conventionally traced to the social and cultural anthropologist's move towards collecting first-hand data on the social life of particular cultures. It is a form of qualitative research usually associated with the disciplines of sociology and anthropology. Typically, the term ethnography refers both to a research process and also to a research product – a cultural portrait of the social system studied (Agar, 1980; Hammersley and Atkinson, 1983). While there is, unsurprisingly, no unanimity as to the definition of ethnography, in practice it does have a number of distinguishing features (Atkinson and Hammersley, 1994; Hammersley and Atkinson, 1983).

Ethnography emphasizes the detailed examination of the nature of particular social phenomena in a very small number of settings; it is not unusual for ethnographic research to be conducted in just one social system. In the social system, ethnographers are committed to being present to the social situation studied as it unfolds, and they attend to the mundane, to the routine, daily habits of mind and behavior (Fetterman, 1998). Researchers interact with those they study primarily through participant observation and unstructured interviewing, creating a set of field notes as their main data documents. They also examine any documents or records that become relevant to the study.

Typically, ethnographers begin data collection without a predetermined set of analytic categories, and focus more narrowly as the study proceeds. Hammersley and Atkinson (1983) refer to this as ethnography's 'funnel' structure – that is its focus narrows over the study. Accordingly, conceptual elements are more likely to be derived from researchers' experience in the field than to be taken into it (Wolcott, 1992). Ethnographic research is further distinguished by the extended period of time that researchers spend in the field. In organization studies, most researchers who refer to their work as 'ethnographic' have made commitments to spend one year in the participant observer role where they take part in the life of the organization and are present to the situations they study (e.g. Barley, 1990; Kunda, 1991). Van Maanen (1998) has discussed this in terms of the need for researchers to be present for an annual cycle within the social system studied and to have invested sufficient time in the setting so that they have learned and are able to comport their behavior to its particular cultural rules. At this point, they can claim to have learned and understood a portion, at least, of the habits of mind and action of members of the social system studied.

For the most part, these research practices are consistent with most field studies. But, as I noted earlier, the term ethnography refers to both a research process and a research product. In the end, ethnographers are distinguished from other field-based researchers by their commitment to produce culturally focused descriptions and interpretations from their experience, enquiry and examination in the field (Wolcott, 1980, 1992).

Grounded theory overlaps to a degree with all of these approaches to qualitative research. While grounded theorists generally do not share action researchers commitments to organizational transformation or to partnering with research subjects in the inquiry process, they are interested in developing theoretical elements that are useful to practitioners in the settings studied, providing them some understanding and control over situations they encounter on a daily basis (Glaser and Strauss, 1967). The originators' studies and theorizing on awareness and dying in medical settings played a role in changing communication practices in those settings. As an approach, though, grounded theory probably has more in common with case studies and with ethnography. Grounded theory shares with more ethnographic approaches a reserved and modest stance towards existing theory and a style of analysis that interweaves data collection and theory building so that, as the research progresses, the analyst successively redefines and narrows her focus of study. However, whereas generally ethnographers are interested in understanding as much as possible about the cultural aspects of the contexts they enter as researchers, grounded theorists may not be so culturally oriented.

Similarly, the grounded theory style of handling and interpreting data may be incorporated into case studies. Post and Andrews (1982) explicitly advocate the grounded theory style of comparative analysis for case study research. And, as I'll discuss later in the book, the grounded theory style of data interpretation has been blended with the case study design and with ethnographic approaches to produce adaptations of this approach to qualitative research.

In closing, this chapter has underscored the extensiveness and the plurality of research perspectives that are expressed in the history, the investigative paradigms, and the research styles of communities of qualitative researcher practitioners. Note, though, that although I have devoted some attention to action research, case studies and ethnography, I have said little about ethnomethodology (Garfinkel, 1967), semiotics (Barley, 1983; Eco, 1976; Manning, 1987), deconstruction (Calas, 1992; Calas and Smircich, 1992; Derrida, 1976, 1978; Kilduff, 1993; Martin, 1990) or discourse and narrative analysis (Bruner, 1991; Burke, 1969; O'Connor, 1996; Phillips and Brown, 1993) as traditions and communities of research practice which have also found expression in management and organizational qualitative research. Many of these approaches are representative of closer ties between the humanities and social sciences, as the flowering of literary theory and cultural studies (begun during the moment of blurred genres) has attracted the interest of scholars in the social sciences (Grant and Fine, 1992). Management and organization scholars, too, have explored these humanities centered areas of concern and their accompanying investigative approaches. The domain of qualitative research is indeed plural if not somewhat confusing to the newcomer.

2

Situating grounded theory within its philosophical, sociological, and personal contexts

Chapter 1's overview of qualitative research took a methodological perspective on the historical, the paradigmatic and the practice contexts of the grounded theory approach. In Chapter 2, my focus shifts to more disciplinary and personally oriented contextual concerns. This chapter begins with the branch of philosophy and social theory that informs grounded theory, providing it a particular perspective on what constitutes social reality and how that reality should be investigated. It then moves on to sketch the theoretical and investigative concerns in sociology during the sixties when the grounded theory approach was articulated. The chapter ends by considering some features of the originators' biographies as they are relevant to the grounded theory style of research.

American pragmatism and the symbolic interactionist school of sociology

American pragmatism and, in particular, sociology's symbolic interactionist school of thought constitute the disciplinary traditions that helped to inform grounded theory. Symbolic interactionism can best be understood as a working through of the pragmatist world view. The set of ideas associated with symbolic interactionism developed from the work of early 20th century American pragmatist philosophers William James, George H. Mead, Charles Pierce, Charles Horton Cooley and John Dewey. These philosophers shared a sense of disenchantment with what they saw as the irrelevance of the philosophy and social sciences of their day to people's every-day lived situations. They wanted to develop a way of thinking about and conceptualizing human behavior that focused attention on people's practices and their lived realities; they shared the objective of understanding social life 'in the making,' as it was created (Prus, 1996). Cooley and Mead, for example, both saw social life as process, and they underscored the centrality of interaction to bonding people together in groups (Prus, 1996).

As Rock (1979) explains, the framing of life as social process carries over to the pragmatist view of knowledge. Pragmatism conceives of knowledge as an experiential process rather than a mirror of some independent reality. Because knowledge is experiential, the reality that is composed, whether by social researchers or other social actors, shifts as it is built up in transaction with the world and with others in it. Thus, knowledge generated by social researchers can never be complete or confident, but when grounded in particular experiences, it can possess a limited authenticity. Pragmatism recognizes a domain of knowledge in which a knowledge or understanding *of events* is possible by focusing attention on them and rendering them problematic. This knowledge derives from intimate acquaintance with the events studied and from close experiential connections with them.

In fact, the American pragmatists all emphasized the symbolic and social character of human thought and behavior as well as the importance of close connection with the subjects and situations under study. Mead, who is generally viewed as the primary originator of the ideas that comprise the symbolic interactionist perspective, was concerned with acknowledging and articulating the role that subjective experience played in social interaction. Accordingly, the proposition that human beings have a sense of self that we develop through interaction with others is at the core of Mead's theoretical framework. It is through the sense of self that as humans we are able to construct the actions that we will take towards the objects in our world (Mead, 1934). For example, my sense of myself as a 'manager' grows out of the actions and interactions I engage in. Thus, it is shaped by the kinds of work that I do, by the nature of my interactions with others who are 'subordinates' and so on. Furthermore, my sense of self as 'manager' will shape the actions I take and my interactions with others.

This concern with subjective experience, while consistent with the phenomenological school of philosophy, was at odds with prevailing behaviorist notions that human behavior could be explained through the observation and operation of observable external stimuli alone. For Mead, it was necessary to understand the meaning those external stimuli held for people in order to understand their behavior. For example, as 'manager' what is the meaning I make of 'subordinates.' Mead saw individuals as acting in a social context in which we ascribe meaning to objects and actions, and base our own actions on those construed meanings. Mead believed constructed meaning systems provided the key to understanding the link between individuals and the society (Layder, 1994).

The notion of meaning and its influence on social behavior is the central and critical idea in the symbolic interactionist position. Humans' interaction with the world is mediated through our processes of meaning making and interpretation. With meaning and interpretation as its core concern, symbolic interactionism has clear affinities with the interpretive paradigm discussed in Chapter 1. This understanding of the role of meaning and interpretation was further articulated by Herbert Blumer.

He was one of Mead's pupils at the University of Chicago, where his dissertation titled 'Method in Social Psychology' focused on the methodological implications of the unique status of the subject as meaning maker. Blumer's development of Mead's ideas formulated a research methodology for the tradition he named 'symbolic interactionism.' Blumer (1969) argued that there are three premises on which this tradition rests, and in each of them you see clearly the relationship between meaning and action that the term symbolic interactionism captures (Prasad, 1993).

First, *people interpret the meaning of objects in the world and then act upon those interpretations*, that is, meanings inform and guide action. In this view of the world, objects are conceived very broadly. To provide illustrations from work organizations: objects include physical objects, such as a company uniform, a mission statement, or a policy. Objects can also be social. Particular types of individual, such as quality control inspectors or subordinates, are examples. Social objects also include gestures, as in the case of a fist slamming down onto the top of a table during a meeting, and they extend to social situations such as an awards ceremony. Most importantly, though, social objects include language. If we as researchers are to understand the actions of quality control inspectors, for example, we need to learn the meanings relevant physical, social and verbal objects have for them, and thus to gain insight into their behavior.

Second, *meaning arises from social interaction* – communication between and among individuals – and not from the object. Meaning arises from the social interactions people have with others in their world. Also, because communication is at the core of interaction, the importance of language and other symbolic phenomena is underscored. The classic illustration of this point is Howard Becker's (1953) study of drug use. In this study, the relationship between meaning and interaction is highlighted as Becker came to understand that it was through interaction with other marijuana users that individuals learned how to smoke the drug, how to interpret and respond to its effects, and how to develop connoisseurship. Smoking marijuana only became meaningful through a novice's interactions within a social network of users. A business organization provides another illustration. The meaning of an organizational policy for paid time off is not given in the policy itself, the object. Rather, the meaning arises out of organization member's experience of the policy in the context of communication and interaction with other organization members who engage or have some contact with the policy. As members of an organization, the meaning of this newly introduced 'paid time off' policy will evolve in our interactions as we deal with issues relating to it that arise.

Third, *meaning is handled in and modified through an ongoing interpretive process*. Thus, meaning is not fixed or stable; it is always in process. Actors can select, suspend, and even transform the meanings they hold in light of changing situations and circumstances. The paid time off policy may come to take on a different meaning to a particular group, for example, as a result of that group's members' experience of using the policy to deal with a particular kind of personal circumstance that arises, or as a result of new leadership, etc. Meanings are consequently continuously revised as they serve as a means to guide action.

As did Mead, Blumer, too, focused on the concept of self – our ideas of who we are and our inner experiences. It is our ability to hold a concept of who we are and to take action in light of our view of ourselves that forms the basis for the formulation of meaning and experience. For example, an understanding of myself as an 'employee' will result in a particular way of behaving in the presence of other employees as compared with the presence of managers, and in a particular attitude towards a uniform that I may be required to wear. I will define these social and physical objects through my interaction with them and in light of my view of who I am. Once these objects are defined they can be imbued with meaning and with value. Consequently, according to Blumer, people's actions towards the objects in their world are sensible in light of the meanings and values these objects hold for them. These meanings and values lead to self-directed behavior. Further, because like all objects the self is always subject to reinterpretation, my definition of self can change. New definitions of objects create new definitions of who we are. Suppose, now, that this 'employee' is promoted to 'manager,' then my sense of self will change, and I shall likely find myself acting in very different ways with subordinates who were once peers and colleagues who were once superiors. Similarly, my views on the company uniform may also change. Thus, new experience changes the sense of self, changes the meaning of objects, and thereby leads to changes in behavior.

With the creation of meaning at the core of human behavior, symbolic interactionists view behavior as the result of meaning making or interpretive processes. Social behavior is inherently processual (Blumer, 1969), and it tends towards instability as behavior shifts in the context of revised or different interpretations. Any knowledge generated about such behavior is itself always in process.

Research implication of symbolic interactionism
Clearly, from the perspective of this framework, in order for collective action to take place meaning must be shared. Communication and a common language provide the means for achieving shared meaning. Where there is consensus as to meaning, where individuals learn and share definitions of objects, events and situations, people can plan their behavior with others (Chenitz and Swanson, 1986). Social organization, therefore, is made up of patterns and intertwined lines of action that express common meanings attached to various social objects. These

structures of everyday commonsense meaning (individual and collective) that are disclosed in observable regular styles and patterns of acting towards social objects, then, are regarded by symbolic interactionists as the only reality that sociologists can describe (Rock, 1979).

Symbolic interactionism's most important methodological premise is that all social inquiry must be grounded in the particular empirical world studied. The 'empirical world' is taken to refer to:

> the minute-by-minute, day-to-day social life of individuals as they act together, as they develop understandings and meanings, as they engage in 'joint action' and respond to each other as they adapt to situations, and as they encounter and move to resolve problems that arise through their circumstances. (Woods, 1992: 348)

Blumer argued strongly for first-hand empirical research and, at the same time, he reinforced this by remonstrating against the trend to remove sociologists from intimate familiarity with the life and experience of people in society (Collins and Makowsky, 1978). Indeed, symbolic interactionism has always been regarded by its proponents and practitioners as a research tradition whose particular contribution has been the empirical knowledge generated by its field research as much as its theoretical framework.

Within this tradition, not surprisingly, participant observation, is the research ideal. And, consistent with a concern with meaning and action, behavior is studied at two levels. Symbolic interactionists study behavior at both the interactional or behavioral level and the symbolic level. This, of course, will include detailed observations of behavior in a specific situation as well as focused analysis on the symbolic meaning that is transmitted via action. Less ostensive, the latter requires the researcher to understand behavior as a setting's participants understand it. This results in an overriding concern with the detailed study of behavior as symbolic interactionists pay careful attention to the overt behavior, interactions and situations of those they study. Detailed empiricism is the norm (Denzin, 1989a) and researchers must enter the social worlds of the people they study in order to understand the situation from the subject's point of view and to observe first hand what the subject finds meaningful and how she makes meaning.

This detailed description becomes the foundation from which researchers can formulate an interpretation of the subject's behavior (Blumer, 1969). These interpretations, or 'theories,' constitute researcher translations of what they have observed into the language of their research discipline (Denzin, 1989a); nevertheless, their grounding in and closeness to the data remain.

Although Mead and Blumer have been very active in establishing the overall coherence of symbolic interactionism, the tradition does not comprise a tightly integrated set of ideas. Indeed, a number of other scholars have developed the framework in a number of different directions. Meltzer, Petras and Reynolds (1975) and Prus (1996) point to a more modernist expression of symbolic interactionism amongst researchers from what they term the 'Iowa School.' This modernist turn is reflected in their belief that they are able to accurately capture others' interpretations and in their concern with hypothesis testing and the application of more detached, quantitative information gathering and analytic techniques to access social worlds. On the other hand, Denzin has reformulated a version of symbolic interactionism that underscores researchers' own interpretive acts and develops this school of thought along more postmodern lines. He argues that symbolic interactionism should become more reflexive and interpretive: hence the term interpretive interactionism (Denzin, 1989b). Taking its cue from cultural studies, critical theory and feminist studies, such an interactionism could focus its attention to such topics as power, violence, and ideology.

Grounded theory's association with the symbolic interactionist school of thought is repeatedly articulated by its originators and their students (e.g. Charmaz, 1990; Chenitz and Swanson, 1986; Corbin, 1991; Glaser, 1998; Keddy et al., 1996; Strauss, 1987). It is particularly important for those organization researchers who work outside sociology's disciplinary boundaries to appreciate this link between grounded theory and symbolic interactionism, because the latter's conception of how individual and social reality are created and maintained pervades the approach. As a set of research practices, and often as a research product, grounded theory reflects symbolic interactionism's theoretical and methodological presuppositions about the nature of the social world and the way it can be studied (Layder, 1990). In terms of theoretical suppositions, grounded theorists informed by this school of thought enter any research setting and any research topic oriented towards behavior at the symbolic and interactional levels. This means observing and understanding behavior from the participants' point of view, learning about participants' worlds, learning about their interpretation of self in the context of given interactions, and learning about the dynamic properties of interaction.

In terms of methodological assumptions, the grounded theory approach, indeed the term itself, underscores the symbolic interactionist belief that each and every aspect of the inquiry process must be subject to the 'test of the empirical world and has to be validated through such a test' (Blumer, 1976: 13). Blumer's insistence on keeping faith with the empirical world studied in all aspects of the research process, not only in data collection, is echoed clearly in the grounded theory approach (Woods, 1992). It is echoed in the following beliefs. The kinds of issues appropriate for study are those that are relevant and problematic in the social situation studied. The researcher should enter the research process with as few advance assumptions as possible. The conceptual categories and the broad interpretive frameworks developed should result from the researcher's interaction with and closely conform to the situation studied.

Sociology in the early twentieth century

Symbolic interactionism had become an established school of thought in sociology, especially at the University of Chicago, during the 1920s and 1930s. And during this time, as Chapter 1 indicated, under the influence of Robert Park and also Ernest Bergess, that institution laid the basis of the field research tradition in sociology with its noted urban sociological studies. *The Polish Peasant in Europe and America* was followed by other sociological classics such as Shaw's *Jack-Roller* (1930) and Cressey's *The Taxi Dance Hall* (1932). These studies, and many more like them, established participant observation with its associated practices of conducting extended observations, informal interviewing, and examining documentary materials as a recognized research method in sociology.

During the 1940s and 1950s, however, the Chicago School's preeminent status began to wane with the rise in importance of other institutions. By the mid-1900s, then, the emphasis on first hand detailed empirical investigations of focused social situations which that institution had sponsored was by no means the prevailing model of sociological research. At its theoretical end, as it were, sociology embraced the ideal of grand theoretical schemes generated by sociologists of eminence such as Talcott Parsons. Turner has characterized this time period as exhibiting an 'orthodoxy which saw major theorists as the only possible source of the theoretical insights which has to be checked out by "proletarian testers"' (1988: 111) who were armed with an increasingly sophisticated array of statistical techniques for so doing. Quantitative methods dominated sociology during this period.

Talcott Parsons' work epitomized this theory building in the grand tradition. Parson's formal structural–functional theory, articulated in the 1950s and 1960s, provided a complex multi-level analytic model of social life that described it at a high level of generality and abstraction. In Parson's framework, emphasis was placed on delineating the 'social system.' Society was understood as a complex system of interrelated parts. Its component institutions or structures, for example, politics, economy, religion, education, all serve functions in creating and maintaining society. Parson's structural–functional theory sought to classify the basic functions that must be carried for society to survive. Parson's work, is, indeed, 'high' theory, far distant from the ground of everyday individual behavior, and it is representative of an era in which general theory was to a great extent separated from detailed research (Collins and Makowsky, 1978).

The prominence of this approach in sociology in the mid 1900s, then, formed the context in which Herbert Blumer, with others, initiated a second generation of the Chicago School. Among these others were Everett Hughes, Howard Becker and Anselm Strauss (Woods, 1992). This second Chicago group shared a commitment to getting their hands dirty in direct observation and to developing theory out of their research.

Accordingly, in the preface to *The Discovery of Grounded Theory*, Glaser and Strauss characterize the sociology of this time as struggling with a divide between elaborated theories and empirical research. They critique Parson's theoretical framework as having little application to the reality of people's everyday lives, produced, as it was, less from first-hand empirical investigation and more by thinking through ideas and issues in a reasonably abstract way (Layder, 1994). It was Parson's form of logico-deductive grand theory and other more speculative theories that they saw as stultifying sociology. They sought to redress this form of empirically dissociated theorizing through the development of theory that was grounded in the real world and was relevant to its social actors. In addition, they aimed to produce a text that would not only codify the research practices associated with such a theory but, in achieving this, the text would also legitimate such an approach to research and theory development.

And, they had support in this endeavor. A number of other second-generation Chicago sociologists were also interested in articulating and codifying the interpretive techniques of participant observation into a rigorous research approach (Woods, 1992). One among them was Howard Becker, with whom Strauss had worked on the classic study of medical socialization, *Boys In White* (Becker et al., 1961). Interestingly, from the perspective of this present historical moment, much of this work curiously conflates qualitative and statistical analysis. Becker, for example, at that time suggested that qualitative researchers deal with 'quasi-statistics' and that the conclusions that they may come to through their analytic work are 'implicitly numerical' (1958: 656). (This is a far cry from the way in which Becker currently discusses qualitative research (1992)). Thus, there were others besides Anselm Strauss and Barney Glaser who were also working to bring increased codification to qualitative methods and who provided a supportive context for articulating the grounded theory method. However, there is much to suggest that they were working towards increasing legitimacy for such methods during a time when the language of hypothetico-deductive models and their associated quantitative procedures set the terms for any discussions of method.

The personal contexts of Barney Glaser and Anselm Strauss

Anselm Strauss

Anselm Strauss earned his undergraduate degree in sociology at the University of Virginia. There, he cites as noteworthy two events (Corbin, 1991). The first was his reading of the great sociological monograph *The Polish Peasant in Poland and America* by Thomas and Znaniecki (1918), because it introduced him to fieldwork and a way of theorizing sociologically. The second was his introduction to John Dewey and, through the latter, to pragmatist philosophy.

Strauss went on to graduate school at the University of Chicago in the 1940s where he was exposed to the more humanistic branch of symbolic interactionism that was associated with the 'Chicago School.' Indeed, Strauss is noted as a Chicagoan because he later returned to the school as a faculty member from 1952 to 1958. This intellectual heritage was expressed in a number of ways. The tradition of urban fieldwork set out in the writings of Thomas I. Park and the faculty present at Chicago reinforced in Strauss the need to go out into the field to discover what was really happening; they underscored the value of advocating reform based on careful fieldwork, and stressed the importance of understanding the structural conditions in which social phenomena were situated because it was context that provided meaning.

Herbert Blumer, who was on the faculty at Chicago at the time, introduced Strauss to the work of Mead. In this relationship between Blumer and Strauss, the conceptual and methodological tenets of symbolic interactionism were stressed. Mead's work highlighted to Strauss the importance of interaction, of the symbolic meaning of objects, and of time and social process. And as for himself, Blumer imparted to Strauss the great importance of putting together theory and data. In all his writings, spanning some 50 years, Strauss insists on the primacy of theory. For him, the purpose of research data was to lead to theoretical formulations about social situations as opposed, for example, to providing a set of noteworthy findings.

After graduate school, Strauss again returned to the work of John Dewey – the person to whom he acknowledged his greatest intellectual debt (Strauss, 1987). For it was from Dewey that he derived his sensitivity to action and action schemes, especially action in relation to problematic situations, to the processual nature of events, and to the creative and open ended nature of social reality (Corbin, 1991). When he was back in Chicago as a faculty member, he had the opportunity to work and converse with C. Everett Hughes and with Howard Becker on projects related to organizations, occupations, careers and work.

Strauss had clearly been well immersed in the tradition and practice of fieldwork. Nevertheless, as he carried out his early substantive studies during the late 1940s and through the 1950s, he is described as grappling for analytic procedures that would help him to explicate the elements of action and structural conditions that were becoming thematic in his work (Corbin, 1991).

Barney Glaser
Barney Glaser joined Strauss at the University of California, San Francisco in the early 1960s where a group of sociologists were studying organizations, occupations, policy, science, families, etc. as they related to processes of health (Maines, 1991). Barney Glaser brought to the relationship an interesting background in English as well as his training in sociology. He studied literature and received instruction in 'explication de text' (the close textual reading that we usually associate with literary criticism) at the Sorbonne in Paris. Later, he received his sociological training at Columbia University, where he acquired a background in inductive or discovery oriented quantitative sociology. This was under the influence of Paul Lazarsfeld and Robert Merton. The former was recognized for his contributions to quantitative research techniques and methodology development, especially for the use of multivariate analysis, which allows the analyst to tease out the interactions between theoretical elements. Glaser describes how he was sensitized to the potential for qualitative data to generate concepts by the practice at Columbia at the time of preceding a survey research program with an interview study to help formulate the survey questions that the researcher was interested in exploring. These interview studies generated very rich data whose theoretical implications were under explored (Glaser, 1998).

Merton, on the other hand, was known for the generation of more modest middle range sociological theories within the broad structural–functional framework used by Parsons that, as previously discussed, dominated sociological theorizing at the time. Glaser credits Merton as providing lessons on theoretical coding; specifically with the lesson that substantive concepts had to be related through theoretical codes to generate more general theories. He goes on, however, to note that while Merton provided valuable training on theorizing, this training was in the abstract, for most of his theories were not grounded in social reality (Glaser, 1998). In some respects, then, Barney Glaser was a convert to the symbolic interactionist school of thought, to the procedures of participant observation and to the process of deriving theory from naturalistic empirical investigations. However, he was a convert who brought with him particular training in textual interpretation and in developing theoretical products.

Set against the backdrop of the above discussion of the sociological context, it seems that Glaser and Strauss came together at a time when they had in common a strong dissatisfaction with the nature of theorizing that prevailed in sociology. Similarly, they shared a conviction that theory needed to be intimately connected to rich observational data. I would take this point further, arguing that their primary concern was the development of a different kind of social *theory* – one in which empirical research and theory were tightly coupled – rather than a different kind of research methodology. Accordingly, I believe the title of the *Discovery* book with its emphasis on 'discovery' in relation to achieving a particular kind of conceptual product, 'grounded theory,' reflects this. The research process they articulated, then, provided the means to achieve the development of more empirically grounded theories. The particular combination of their respective intellectual biographies facilitated their working out an approach to data collection, analysis and theory generation that introduced a set of systematic procedures that both extended and supplemented the participant observation research practice. These practices enabled researchers to develop empirically grounded theories of every day action in context.

This Chapter has underscored the relevance of a disciplinary tradition, a school of thought, and personal and professional history to the grounded theory style of qualitative research. Sociology and symbolic interactionism's theoretical tradition equipped its researchers, people like Herbert Blumer, Howard Becker, Anselm Strauss, and Barney Glaser, with a particular perspective, a set of conceptual antecedents, and a preferred investigative strategy that shaped their research.

As researchers, we need to be aware of these in order to fully appreciate the possibilities and limits of our chosen genre of qualitative research practice (LeCompte, Millroy and Preissle, 1993; Wolcott, 1992). Indeed, many researchers would argue that research without these is impossible for we would otherwise not be able to orient ourselves to the stream of actions, events, and words that constitute the empirical worlds qualitative researchers investigate. A theoretical perspective informs how we understand complex social realities and what we direct our attention to when collecting and conceptualizing data (Becker, 1986). In his guide for conducting fieldwork, William Foote Whyte both underscores the importance of having an explicit theoretical perspective and suggests some of the qualities it should posses. He claims

> The first requirement for useful fieldwork and theorizing is to get yourself a good orienting theory. Such a framework guides you toward data that will prove useful in later analysis without focusing the study so narrowly as to exclude data whose importance you do not recognize at the start of your project. (1984: 250)

A good theoretical perspective, such as symbolic interactionism, helps qualitative researchers orient themselves to the worlds they study, but it does not specify what they will find. Increasingly, qualitative researchers in management and organization studies are specifying the schools of thought that provide their orienting theoretical frame. For example, Gephart (1978, 1993) explicitly acknowledges and details the orienting perspective provided by ethnomethodology. Pettigrew (1990) similarly draws attention to and describes his informing theoretical perspective. Using the phrase 'a theory of method' (Pettigrew, 1990: 268) to denote it, he describes the way in which contextualism has provided a theoretical perspective which gives shape to his research (both data gathering and analysis) and theorizing on organizational change.

Part Two

The Grounded Theory Research Approach

——————————— 3 ———————————

Distinguishing characteristics of grounded theories

Having provided a perspective on the context in which *The Discovery of Grounded Theory* was written, in Part Two I shall discuss next the research approach's underlying logic and the research outputs it is directed towards achieving. The key operational features of the approach as well as developments in research practice that have occurred over the last 30 years are described. Here in Chapter 3, I begin by sketching the broad features of the grounded theory approach. Following this, I spend some time clarifying the theoretical outcomes, namely a grounded theoretical framework, the approach is intended to achieve, and identify the key language terms through which its theoretical elements are described. The chapter ends with a consideration of grounded theory's applicability to the development of process theories – an area of current research interest in studies of management and organization.

As I have indicated, the procedural logic of the grounded theory approach was initially articulated in 1967 and in the originators' substantive publications of dying in medical institutions. These were the very studies in which the approach and research practices were worked out (e.g. Glaser and Strauss, 1965b). The original methodological monograph was written as a polemic against hypothetico-deductive, speculative theory-building and its associated research practices that characterized the sociological context of the time. This polemical focus is reflected in the book's specific purposes. These are stated as: to encourage researchers to use their intellectual imagination and creativity to develop theories relating to their areas of inquiry; to suggest methods for doing so; to offer criteria to evaluate the worth of discovered theory; and to propose an alternative rhetoric, that of generation, to balance out the rhetoric of justification featured in journal articles and monographs.

Given these purposes, its discussions of research operations are not always as fully developed as a novice qualitative researcher might like. As the authors were at the time centrally concerned with proposing an alternative form of sociological theory, the reader has to work her way through their presentations and critique of a variety of research and theory building approaches to find operational details of the approach. Its logic and distinguishing characteristics, though, are clearly articulated.

Grounded theory's distinctive features, as initially presented, are its commitment to research and 'discovery' through direct contact with the social world studied coupled with a rejection of *a priori* theorizing. This does not mean, however, that researchers should embark on their studies without the general guidance provided by some sort of orienting theoretical perspective. It does mean that they should bring preconceived constructs and hypotheses to their data gathering and analysis. The rejection of pre-conceived theories is argued vehemently by the originators in the original monograph specifically because, as Glaser and Strauss claim, such theories have the effect of obstructing the development of theory by coming between researchers and the subjects of their study. When this eschewal of pre-existing theories is combined with an emphasis on research and 'discovery,' it results in a conception of knowledge as *emergent*. Knowledge is composed by researchers in the context of investigative practices that afford them intimate contact with the subjects and phenomena under study.

Grounded theory is entirely consistent with its symbolic interactionist heritage in terms of both research practice and research focus in its insistence on direct contact with the social world studied and in its attention to symbols and behavior, respectively. However, it distinguishes itself from this tradition in its particular analytic extensions of and supplements to participant observation. Indeed, as I suggested in Chapter 2, one of the objectives that Glaser and Strauss pursue in their original publication is to make the operational strategies and interpretive practices of qualitative research (specifically participant observation) more systematic in order to make the links between qualitative, natural data and formal theory much more explicit. Certainly, the formal vocabulary of grounded theory lends a more systematic and rigorous tone to this variation of qualitative field research.

Grounded theory as research product: a perspective on theory

As the title of the original monograph suggests, it is fundamentally concerned with the development of empirically grounded theory. Unlike some sociologists working in the symbolic interactionist tradition, who at the time felt that researchers should concentrate their research attention on describing the concrete empirical worlds they were studying rather than on generating theories (Rock, 1979), Glaser and Strauss (1967) argued that sociologists must generate formal theories out of their research data in order to advance understanding of the social world. The theorizing process, though, begins with the creation of theories that are substantive in nature.

In *The Discovery of Grounded Theory*, Glaser and Strauss make much of the difference between substantive and formal theory. They view formal theory as the sociologist's goal. However, to be valid, they insist that it be developed from a substantive grounding in concrete social situations. They offered the following distinctions between the two:

> By substantive theory we mean that developed for a substantive, or empirical, area of sociological inquiry, such as patient care, race relations, professional education, delinquency, or research organizations. By formal theory, we mean that developed for a formal, or conceptual, area of sociological inquiry , such as stigma, deviant behavior, formal organization, socialization . . . (1967: 32).

Thus, substantive theory is prior to formal theory, and it is closely linked to the practice domain. It represents the close connection to empirical reality that the originators and others working in the Chicago tradition were arguing for in the 1960s. In management and organization studies, many of our theories are substantive in nature: decision-making and leadership, are two instances of such theories. Today, substantive theories might be developed for issues associated with working in virtual organizations or managing contingent workers. When we speak of formal theory, however, we usually refer to those areas of inquiry that operate at a high level of generality, such as systems theory, agency theory, population ecology, and contingency theory.

In Glaser and Strauss's view, substantive and formal theory are clearly related. Substantive theory can provide a link to more formal theory, but this is achieved by working empirically to develop conceptual categories at higher levels of abstraction and generality. But, what is a theory, substantive, formal, grounded or otherwise? Although, as I just indicated, the original monograph does dedicate considerable space to clarifying the difference between substantive and formal theory, the emphasis there is on the distinction between 'substantive' and 'formal.' The notion of 'theory,' by contrast, seems to be taken for granted, perhaps presuming a shared understanding on the part of its readers. There is a little irony to this given that many criticisms of analyses that are presented as grounded theories revolve around concerns that they are not developed theories (Wilson and Hutchinson, 1996).

The understanding of theory reflected in Glaser and Strauss's methodological and substantive work is consistent with the received scientific view of theory. From this perspective, the theories they appear to have in mind can be conceived as a linguistic mechanism or language term composed by researchers that organizes and describes an empirical world (Bacharach, 1989) through a constructed set of interrelated propositions that enables researchers to make sense out of observed events. Denzin's (1989a) discussion, which reflects this received view of theory, argues that this mechanism organizes the world through a set of concepts that forms a conceptual scheme. It is concepts that define and shape the content of theories providing a new way of viewing the world. Concepts bring order to the world expressed in data documents, highlighting what things go together and what things are distinct from each other (Patton, 1981).

Interestingly, as Denzin (1989a) also points out, this new way of organizing and perceiving the world has a double meaning; a concept provides a new way to look at the world at the same time as it brings some aspect of the world into existence through conceptualization. The descriptive world captured in researchers' field notes, interview transcripts, and documents is given an organization, a shape and an overall coherence that could not be perceived before the act of conceptualization. As an illustration, one of Glaser and Strauss's earlier concepts was that of a 'non-scheduled status passage' (Glaser and Strauss, 1965a). This concept composes and brings into focus the patterns of action and interaction that ensue from timing issues associated with the dying process.

Further, these concepts can be either descriptive or they can be relational. Descriptive concepts show what the theory is about. Relational concepts, on the other hand, specify observable relationships, and the relationships between concepts are described through propositions or hypotheses. The specification of relationships among concepts is critical to the ability of a theory to offer an account of how things happen. For example, a study of managers in action may yield a number of descriptive concepts that capture different managerial styles. However, without relating the styles to other elements, whether they be managers' perspectives on themselves, to conditions in their work contexts, to particular consequences, and so on, the study essentially will remain at a relatively thin theoretical level. It will not have the explanatory power to account for the styles of managerial action in the settings studied. The importance of a theory's ability not only to explain, but also to tell a 'story' is underscored by Maxwell (1998). He insists that a useful theory will tell an enlightening story about some aspect of the world, providing insight into and broader understanding of it.

In hypothetico-deductive models of research, the line of investigative action begins with theory; it moves from the definition of concepts and their proposed relations out to the 'real world' where, according to the theory, they ought to be observed and where they are tested. In the grounded theory model, the line of investigative action is reversed. It moves from empirical observation to the definition of concepts. Figure 3.1 depicts this contrast. As a research approach, the set of practices that comprise the grounded theory style of research are designed to help researchers make the move from empirical observation to composing

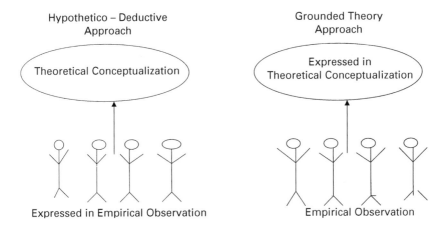

Figure 3.1   *Contrasting the line of investigative action in hypothetico-deductive and grounded theory approaches*

conceptual categories and to delineating the ways in which the categories relate to each other. For researchers executing this move, the creative opportunity and the particular challenge of working within the grounded theory style is that they have to invent some aspect of the social world through their conceptualization. The conceptualized element then becomes a lens for bringing into focus the patterning perceived in the social situation they studied.

Now, development of such conceptual schemes is a fairly ambitious undertaking. And, interestingly, the nature and status of theories developed by researchers has been an issue of discussion and debate in management and organization studies (on the western side of the Atlantic, at least) (Elsbach et al., 1999; Weick, 1999). A number of scholars have confirmed the need for scholars and researchers to develop strong theories in the received definition given above (Bacharach, 1989; Pfeffer, 1993; Sutton and Staw, 1995; Whetten, 1989). At the same time, however, other organization scholars and theorists have taken a more tolerant and inclusive position on what constitutes theory. For example, DiMaggio offers several renditions of what a theory and its value might be. In addition to the received view, theory may be a process narrative or theory might comprise theoretical elements as devices of 'sudden enlightenment' (1995: 391). Also, he points to the garbage can model of organizational choice (Cohen et al., 1972) as an instance of a theoretical hybrid that is part process theory and part enlightenment device.

The notion of theory as a device for potential enlightenment is addressed by Howard Becker (1992) in a discussion of imagery and research. It is a discussion that recognizes central aspects of the interpretive approach, especially the central role played by language in theorizing. Becker cites his teacher's (the symbolic interactionist Herbert

Blumer) insistence that the fundamental operation in researching a phenomenon is 'the production and refinement of an image of the thing we are studying' (Becker, 1992: 210–211). Blumer insisted to Becker that as researchers we are always asking ourselves the following questions: 'What do we think we are looking at? What is its character? More importantly, given what we think it is, is the way we study it and report our findings congruent with that character?' (Becker, 1992: 210). The lesson I take from Becker's comments on this guidance is a twofold one. First, we researchers should pay close attention to the underlying metaphor in the language terms that comprise our theoretical products. Second, a potential contribution can be made by developing a theoretical product that expresses a different underlying metaphor for a phenomenon; this offers the potential for enlightenment. As an illustration, recently in the domain of organization and management, Czarniawska and Joerges (1996) proposed that in our theoretical conversations about how innovations travel, we should replace the concept of 'diffusion' with that of 'translation.' They argue that the social imagery evoked by the latter offers the potential for greater insight into the processes by which ideas travel than does the physical imagery evoked by the diffusion concept. The former better captures the character of the processes. A theoretical product, then, might be a good or a better image for a phenomenon we are studying, expressed as a concept.

The above discussion suggests that we take a fairly inclusive position on just what a theoretical product might be. Weick (1995) underscores this same position when he draws on Merton to note that research products that are labeled theories are really approximations of them. Furthermore, Weick argues that such approximations are entirely consistent when you take a view of theory as a process and the resulting theoretical elements as in-process accomplishments. From Weick's process perspective, theory work can take a number of forms, and it includes such activities as 'abstracting, generalizing, relating, selecting, explaining, synthesizing and idealizing' (1995: 389). The emergent products of these processes may not be formal theories. Nevertheless, they do have a value in summarizing progress made towards understanding a phenomenon, in providing direction for inquiry, and in serving as place markers. As the preceding indicates, my position is that there is room in grounded theory research in management and organization studies for a variety of theoretically oriented products.

Analytic generalizability

It is useful when considering the theoretical outcomes of this research approach to distinguish between statistical generalization and what Yin (1994) has discussed as 'analytic generalization.' As I mentioned earlier, in the hypothetico-deductive approach, the researcher moves from *a priori* definition of concepts and their proposed relationships to their empirical investigation. The issue of statistical generalizability addresses the inferences that can be made about those concepts and their relations in a population on the basis of empirical information collected from a sample. That is, the extent to which investigators might make claims about the plausibility of the theoretical framework for a particular population of subjects based on their testing of it in an appropriate sample of that population.

In the theory building mode, by contrast, where researchers move from empirical observation to the development of concepts and their proposed relations, claims are made about the plausibility of the theorized elements – not about the extent of their expression in a population. Thus, researchers work to generalize the empirical observations they have collected in a linguistic device, namely, their conceptual categories and framework. A conceptual category has analytic generalizability when it can plausibly account for a large number and range of empirical observations. Glaser and Strauss (1967) speak of this when they describe a theory as being generally applicable.

Clarifying the language of grounded theory's theoretical products

The language that Glaser and Strauss use to describe theoretical accomplishments includes the terms, 'categories,' 'core categories,' 'properties,' and 'generalized relations' or 'hypotheses.' And, from their perspective a grounded theory is made up of a number of conceptual categories that are organized in terms of their relationship to each other.

Conceptual categories, properties, and their proposed relations
When Glaser and Strauss (1967) speak of categories, they are using the term synonymously with concepts such as that of the non-scheduled status passage previously described. Similarly, when they write of generalized relations, or hypotheses, they are describing the proposed relations between conceptual categories. Although Whetten (1989) suggests that the term hypothesis be reserved for measured relationships between concepts, Glaser and Strauss (1967) use the terms generalized relations and hypotheses (in later writings, propositions, too) interchangeably.

In the language of grounded theory, conceptual categories and their properties appear to differ in that categories are 'stand alone' elements of the theoretical framework whereas properties are a conceptual element of the category. There appears to be some ambiguity associated with the term, as later writings introduce other terms, for example, dimensions and subcategories, that also seem to point to theorized subelements of a larger conceptual category. What does seem consistent is the idea that there are larger conceptual categories and there are the pieces out of which the category is constructed. So, non-scheduled status passage is the larger conceptual category, and it is constituted through a number of conceptual elements. Further, the more properties or pieces a particular conceptual category possesses, the more fully described or theoretically dense it is. Glaser and Strauss offer the following illustration of these two theoretical elements taken from one of their studies on dying:

> ... two categories of nursing care are the nurse's 'professional composure' and their 'perceptions of social loss' ... that is their view of what degree of loss his death will be to his family and occupation. One property of the category of social loss is 'loss rationales' – that is, the rationales nurses use to justify to themselves their perceptions of social loss. (1967: 36)

Thus, when Glaser and Strauss observed and analyzed the behavior of nurses in the dying situation, they noticed and conceptualized a number of characteristic features. These included a concern with maintaining professional composure and the invocation of justifications regarding the patient's passing. Furthermore, these features could be explained by taking into account the perceived and articulated social significance of the particular patient's death. For example, the death of a mother with young children was commented on in terms that suggested that it held more social significance or loss-value than that of a 95-year old widow. And, in this study, social loss is the 'core' category – that is the conceptual category that is most densely developed, which is most persistent and which accounts for most of the patterns of behavior observed. The theoretical framework they developed from these elements also comprises proposed relations among these categories and their properties – that is, it makes a set of statements about how the conceptualized events in the dying world are related. Specifically, it suggests that the categories of social loss and professional composure and the property of loss rationale are related in a particular way and illustrated in Figure 3.2.

As Figure 3.2 indicates, social loss has a consequence on the nursing staffs' professional composure. With the death of a patient who is perceived as being a high social loss, the nursing staff's ability to maintain their professional composure is in jeopardy. In these situations, the nurses will use loss rationales to explain her death, mediating the

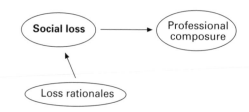

Figure 3.2 *Relationship between the theoretical elements in the social loss framework*

perceived social loss and mitigating the impact on professional composure.

Grounded theory and process

It should by now come as no surprise that from the perspective of those trained in the symbolic interactionist tradition, one way of thinking about sociology is as the study of 'people doing things together' (Becker, 1986). Accordingly, grounded theories as originally conceived are very much oriented towards micro level processes reflected in action and interaction. The researcher focuses on the study of patterns of behavior and meaning which account for variation in interaction around a substantive problem in order to arrive at conceptually based explanations for the processes operating within the substantive problem area.

As a heuristic device, the distinction can be made between research that attends to 'units' as opposed to 'processes' (Bigus et al., 1982). Looking at Glaser and Strauss's dying studies, this focus on process rather than units is quite evident. To illustrate, in *A Time for Dying* (Glaser and Strauss, 1968), the second substantive monograph produced using the grounded theory mode of analysis, process is explicated in two ways. First, the core theoretical category presented in this work is that of a 'trajectory.' This is certainly a process oriented category in that it highlights changes over time, describing how hospitalized sick patients move through various phases towards their deaths. A process orientation is also evident, though, in the description of the interactions and structural conditions that comprise these phases and that stimulate movement from one phase to the next. Process is highlighted in descriptions of the internal mechanics of interaction, their variation, their consequences – themselves promoting further developments in action – and also how they change over time. They did not focus on more static units, for example potential population units such as 'the dying patient' or organizational units such as 'the geriatric ward.'

In works that were to follow the original monograph, Glaser emphasized the attention that researchers ought to be paying to social processes by introducing a theoretical construct called 'basic social process' or 'BSP' (Glaser, 1978). Indeed, he and his colleagues argued that sociology would be advanced by identifying and elaborating theories of generic social processes, the idea being to create theories that capture action unfolding. They identify the 'becoming' process, as in 'becoming' a drug user or perhaps even 'becoming' a manager as an example of one such generic and socially pervasive process (Bigus et al., 1982). 'Deciding' is, of course, another such process. These are examples of more psychologically oriented social processes, but there are also those that focus on social structure in motion. These include bureaucratization, routinization, integration, and so on (Glaser, 1978).

Recently, management and organization researchers have been expressing an increased interest in process oriented theories (Ropo et al., 1997). Researchers are describing process oriented research in various ways – but all reflecting a common element, namely time. For example, Andrew Pettigrew, whose work has reflected a strong process orientation for several decades, speaks of it as being concerned with the dynamics of human action in organizations. He defines process as 'a sequence of individual and collective events, actions and activities unfolding over time in context' (Pettigrew, 1997: 338). Similarly, for Langley (1999: 692), processual research investigates 'events, activities, and choices, ordered over time.' Pentland (1999) takes a slightly different position, suggesting that processual research is concerned with stories as abstract conceptual models that explain sequences of events.

All of these understandings of processual research share a focus on managerial and organizational realities as they move and change in real time. These notions of movement and change are central to the concern with time that is featured in current management conversations of process oriented research. Interestingly, there are echoes of pragmatist interactionist thinking in many of these current statements about process oriented research and theorizing. For example, Pettigrew's comment that 'Human conduct is perpetually in a process of becoming. The overriding aim of the process analyst, therefore, is to catch this reality in flight' (1997: 338) reflects the pragmatist objective to understand social life in the making. Not surprisingly, the use of qualitative methods that allow the researcher to inspect first hand this reality in the making have figured prominently in this form of theorizing.

It is worth noting, by way of bringing this discussion of process to a close, that while Glaser and Strauss (1967) argue that the grounded theory style of research is especially suited to generating theories of social process, they do comment that the method can be used to generate static models – a typology, for example. So, while its informing school of thought orient and make the approach particularly suited to the development of process theories that account for how things happen in social settings, its analytic approach can support the researcher in interpreting and conceptualizing social units found in the research situation. To take the substantive example of contingent workers, a unit oriented researcher might enter a work situation that featured contingent workers and develop conceptual elements that capture all the features or properties of being a contingent worker in that setting. On the other hand, a researcher informed by the symbolic interactionist school of thought would be more likely to attend to processes that are a feature of life as a contingent worker, for example, such as negotiating a workplace identity.

Chapter 3 has highlighted the basic characteristics of the grounded theory approach, focusing particular attention on what the 'theory' in grounded theory refers to. With this understanding of the research approach's end product in mind, Chapter 4 now moves to consider its basic operational practices.

4

Grounded theory's research practices

Chapter 4 introduces the research operations that are at the heart of the grounded theory approach. The assignment of meaning through the activities of naming and comparing is one of the foundational operations, and it is explained. This discussion is followed by the second foundational operation, theoretical sampling. Chapter 4 closes by considering criteria that Glaser and Strauss suggest for evaluating the goodness of researchers composed theoretical products.

In terms of research practice, grounded theory addresses the analytic operations in the qualitative research project. It, accordingly, makes a number of assumptions about the underlying scheme of design that governs how the research study will unfold. It assumes, for example, that researchers are clear as to their purposes for the study, the issues they hope to illuminate, and perhaps the practices it might influence (Maxwell, 1998). Related to this, the grounded theory approach presumes that researchers have arrived at their research question. Furthermore, for the newcomer to qualitative researcher who likely will have addressed the above questions in other methodological designs, grounded theory does not address qualitative research's data gathering operations. While the sampling issues that attend data gathering are considered at length and are integral to the approach's analytic logic, the mechanisms of gathering data observations and composing data documents that become the raw material for analysis are largely ignored.

As such, the grounded theory approach presumes competence in what Van Maanen (1995) refers to as the first 'moment' or activity stage associated with qualitative field-based research – that is with information or data gathering techniques. Glaser and Strauss of course relied on the mainstay of symbolic interactionist research, participant-observation, in their own work. Glaser and Strauss do not explicitly discuss the requisite skills that support the creation of a good set of data documents from field observations, interviews or archival materials. Those practices associated with making and translating systematic observations into field notes, with composing interview questions and transcribing responses, and with reading various kinds of text for the social processes embedded in them are not addressed. This competence is presumed, and novice researchers will have to go to other sources for guidance on these operational practices (e.g. Agar, 1980; Burgess, 1984; Chenitz, 1986;

Hodder, 1994; Lofland and Lofland, 1984; McCracken, 1988; Rubin and Rubin, 1995; Schatzman and Strauss, 1973; Spradley, 1979, 1980; Swanson, 1986a).

That said, while little advice as to data gathering practices is given, Glaser and Strauss do advocate what is now called 'triangulation,' that is collection of data from multiple sources that all are relevant to the studied phenomenon. Examples would include data from semi-structured interviews, from field-observations and from archival sources. In their original monograph, this practice is described as gathering 'slices of data' (Glaser and Strauss, 1967: 65) because different data sources provide different vantage points, as it were, from which to understand a potential conceptual category.

Assigning meaning: constant comparison

The Discovery of Grounded Theory expresses its discussion of how researchers assign meaning to the observations expressed in their data documents in terms of the constant comparative method. This set of practices – which they define as the joint coding and analysis of data – offers a logic for composing conceptual elements that hinges on their articulation through close reading, comparison, and attendant conceptualization of data. These practices follow the concept-indicator model of theory development (Glaser, 1978). That is, concepts are developed that account for perceived patterns in sets of data observations; each concept is indicated by a set of empirical observations. The constant comparative method is conceptualized and described in terms of four stages which span the entire study, moving from assigning meaning to incidents of recorded data to refining and writing up the completed theoretical framework. Each of these stages is characterized by a slightly different form and focus of analytic activity. These described stages are: comparing incidents applicable to each category; integrating categories and their properties; delimiting the theory; and writing the theory (Glaser, 1965; Glaser and Strauss, 1967).

Further, the original monograph introduces memoing as a reflexive practice that helps researchers to articulate and conserve their sense-making about what is going on in the data. Memoing conserves and facilitates sense-making in many different ways through each of the constant comparative process's four forms of analytic activity. It helps to capture ideas as and when they strike, to develop lines of thought about what is happening in the data, to transition between the emerging theoretical framework and existing relevant disciplinary theory, and it is a vehicle to compose initial drafts of documents to be submitted for publication.

While these stages suggest a certain linear progression in the analytic task – each stage is successively transformed into the next – researchers would be setting themselves up for disappointment if they expected analysis to advance according to a linear pattern. Indeed, Glaser and Strauss underscore that iteration is a feature of the approach, and that all stages are in operation throughout the analysis. Consequently, new conceptual categories may be created at any stage of the theory development process.

Stage 1: comparing incidents applicable to each category
In this first form of analytic activity, researchers aim to assign to multiple data observations a common meaning that is captured or composed in a conceptual category. Attention and focus are directed towards drafting categories from the observations in data documents. To do this, as researchers, we take as our beginning point the data incidents that have been collected from observations, interviews, and/or archival material with a view to understanding a particular substantive problem.

In the interest of staying close to the social situation we are studying and of allowing examination of the data to fully inform our conceptualizations, researchers are urged to temporarily suspend from our thinking all preconceived notions, expectations, and any previous theorizing related to the substantive area. Recall that this exhortation reflects the originating authors' dissatisfaction with the grand theoretical schemes that dominated sociology at the time. Their particular concern, therefore, was that researchers not walk into the research situation with ready-to-hand conceptual elements or specific propositions that had not been developed through careful empirical observations. Of course, it is impossible for the researcher to approach her observations *tabla rasa*, and Glaser and Strauss did not intend researchers enter the field without the benefit of training in a disciplinary tradition such as sociology or management and organization theory. Nor, as I've made clear, did they intend that researchers enter the field without the orientation provided by a broad school of thought. Rather, they suggested that we should deliberately hold in abeyance existing ways of thinking about the substantive area we are investigating so as to preclude their prematurely giving form to the data.

In urging this, Rennie (2000) argues that Glaser and Strauss incorporated into their approach the phenomenological technique known as bracketing. Through bracketing, as researchers, we work to surface and examine our biases and pre-existing theoretical commitments specifically so that we can 'bracket' them out. Bracketing, thus, prepares investigators to be able to carefully and critically examine our subject and to suspend our interpreting beliefs (Cohen, 1987). This self-conscious suspension of biases that may prematurely shape the conceptual categories helps analysts to focus attention on our data incidents and to think creatively about what they might mean.

When researchers engage their data during this and the other forms of the constant comparative method, they basically participate in two activities, naming data incidents and comparing data incidents and names. The term 'coding' is introduced in the original monograph (and continues into subsequently published methodological manuscripts) to denote the naming and comparing activities that constitute the constant comparative method. (The word 'coding' also has various other uses, and as a term it becomes increasingly unclear over time. For example, Strauss (1987) suggests that the word be considered as a noun with a code being the product of any analytic activity. Later, as Lonkila (1995) indicates, Strauss and Corbin (1990) seem to use the term to denote the conceptual label attached to a category. And, with the advent of computer assisted software analysis programs, the word code seems to denote a label used for retrieval.) Naming and comparing activities are complemented by a third, supportive activity, memoing. Let us consider each of these.

Naming In naming, researchers attempt to conceptualize and develop abstract meaning for the observations or incidents in their data documents by articulating what they perceive is happening or is being expressed in those incidents. We study an incident in our data set; this may be an observed exchange recorded in field notes, a sentence in an interview transcript, or a phrase in a document. This incident is named, and its name or label represents our interpretation of what is happening in that incident. Furthermore, in very early stages, a given data incident is named in as many different ways as we can extrapolate from it. This brainstorming of possible interpretations pushes us to think broadly about the possible meaning of the incident. (Its 'ultimate' meaning will be settled over the course of the analysis through comparison with other data observations.)

This is the first step in the act of creating a conceptual category that provides a new way of looking at the world. Glaser and Strauss use the word coding to describe this process of composing a name for what is happening in a particular fragment of data, offering little further elaboration other than data incidents are coded into categories. They suggest that this coding (or naming as I prefer to call it) can be done either casually, so to speak, in the margins of field notes or interview transcripts or more formally on index cards. They also point out that researchers need to record what comparison individuals and/or group are involved in the incident.

Comparing Comparing occurs in tandem with naming and is critical to the act of creating conceptual categories for two reasons. First, it helps researchers to develop a common name or category for multiple observations or incidents in the data, pushing us to create more general conceptual categories. Second, it supports the act of naming conceptual categories by helping us to sharpen and clarify what we perceive in our data. So, as analysts, we compare data incidents with other data incidents, and we also compare data fragments with our named working conceptual categories. The process of looking at what is similar and different in the data incidents and of examining the category we created in light of them helps us to clarify what we view as uniform and stable in the data. This can then be reflected in how we name the conceptual categories. Researchers are thus always moving from examination of data incidents to conceptualization and back to data incidents again.

Let us recreate these activities as Glaser and Strauss might have engaged them in their development of a particularly well known concept. It could go something like the following. Researchers scrutinize a data fragment in their field notes that represents a nurse's response to the death of a patient. It reads something like, 'What a loss, he wanted to be a teacher!' How might this data fragment be coded? How might we put a name to what might be expressed in this incident? Some possibilities that might come to mind are 'death as loss' and 'unfulfilled aspirations.' Or, perhaps we might think about whether his aspiration to be a teacher rather than, say, a race car driver is significant. And, if we think that is important, we might try a label or name like 'society is denied a contribution.' You may be thinking of others.

Then, as researchers, we might find and also look for other situations in our data or through further data collection that capture nurses' responses to the death of patients. Other response to other deaths with which that incident might subsequently be compared could include comments like, 'Well, at age 85 with 11 grandchildren, he had a full life,' or 'She has four little children, what will happen to them now that she is gone.' How might these be named? Do any of the existing labels apply? How are they similar to or different from the first hypothetical data incident?

To highlight the process of comparison, let us put these three hypothetical data incidents together and look at them closely, comparing them with each other:

'What a loss, he wanted to be a teacher!'
'Well, at age 85 with 11 grandchildren, he had a full life!'
'She has four little children, what will happen to them now that she is gone'

Now, let us compare them with the initial labels developed to name what might plausibly be expressed in the data:

Death as loss
Unfulfilled aspirations
Society is denied a contribution

At first pass, all the incidents seem to be able to be accommodated under the 'Death as loss' label because they all seem to address the issue of what the patient's death means. Certainly the first and the third data incident also point to the idea of some person or group being denied something that was suggested by the label 'Society is denied a contribution.' So, by comparing the incidents with each other and with the initial labels, an examination of data incidents for what is similar will likely reinforce the idea that the nurses are assigning a value-related meaning to the death of their patients. Over time, by scrutinizing, comparing and thinking about incidents, that idea that nurses variously construe death in terms of its social consequences might well stabilize and be articulated with a more refined word or phrase. Glaser and Strauss, of course, gave the name, 'social loss' to this category.

At the same time as these data incidents are compared for what is similar across them, they are also compared for what is different. Clearly, the second data incident is distinctive in that the passing of the 85 year old man seems to have less import. While comparison highlights what is similar across incidents, it also brings into focus what might be different – the extent of the perceived loss to the individuals, their family, and society at large seems to vary. This difference points to various properties of the category. So, as many incidents are categorized as social loss, our analytic comparisons might suggest that while they all have the quality of social loss in common, there seem to be differences in the representations of social loss. Some of the incidents, such as the mother with young children, may indicate a significant sense of loss. The death of the 85 year old man, however, may be construed as a lower loss.

Comparison may also suggest that these differences may be related to particular features of the individuals that hospital staff are attending to. So, by comparing the data incidents and whether they fall under the 'high' or 'low' property of social loss, we will likely be able to discern the patient characteristics that earn particular valuations on the part of the nursing staff. This process prompts us to begin thinking about other theoretical properties of the category, for example, how hospital staff arrive at a determination of loss, the conditions under which loss will be high, or low, or might change, and so on. The hypothetical data incidents created above certainly point to age as being relevant in the determination of social loss. This recognition would, in its own turn, prompt searching for and comparison of many more expressions of age in order to understand and articulate the role that age might play in determining social loss. Thus, the comparative process refines the conceptual category, and helps to fill out and develop the robustness of the category such as its properties and the conditions under which those properties may be more pronounced or minimized.

To the extent that such valuations on the part of nursing staff are a recurrent feature of what happens when a patient dies, as researchers, we will find many such data incidents to analyze, compare, and code, and many variations on the social loss theme. This means that this category is able to account for much of the data relevant to the way in which hospital staff manage such situations. This is what Glaser and Strauss mean when they claim that any conceptual category must earn its way into the researcher's in-process theoretical framework – the data incidents which point to it must be persistent and recurrent in the data.

Glaser and Strauss recount the research history of their study of how nurses respond to the dying situation in terms that suggest that the category 'social loss' was conceived and so labeled very early on. This may certainly have been the case. In fact, it is fairly common to have observations in the first data documents that point to what will become the core category for the study. However, it is not routine for researchers to be able to crystallize and definitively name that core category during the early phases of the study. Researchers should be wary of entering into analysis with this presumption, expecting instead to arrive at their categories through an iterative, messy and ambiguity-laden process.

Interestingly, Glaser and Strauss (1967) claim that there are two kinds of descriptive category that researchers will be prompted to create from the data: those that we construct in our own language and those that have been created out of the language of the research situation. They suggest that 'social loss' illustrates a category created by the researchers whereas 'composure' demonstrates a category created out of the language of the research situation. The word 'composure', as in 'losing my composure . . . maintaining my composure,' was repeatedly used by nurses. It, too, became one of the conceptual categories that was formulated in this study of the way in which nurses responded to dying in hospitals. Further, they go on to argue that the categories that have been created from the language of the research situation will tend to represent the situated social processes and behaviors that require explanation, and they suggest that the specific language, e.g. composure, represents the local labels for those processes. On the other hand, they maintain that the categories constructed by analysts will provide the explanations for those processes. In other words, recurring language terms in the social situation will point to the problems that actors in the social situation contend with and highlight for researchers what we need to account for, while the categories we articulate in our own terms should explain them. Thus, the behavior of maintaining composure is a central dimension in how nurses personally and professionally handle the dying situation, and it can be explained through the concept of social loss.

Memoing   During stage 1, writing memos is reported as taking two forms. During the initial reading of, say, field notes, writing a memo on an idea that has been sparked by a particular of an incident in the field note margins captures that idea as well as notes an illustration of it. It supports researcher efforts to name what we believe is expressed in the data incidents, helping us to articulate and draft our conceptual categories. A little further into the process of developing categories, as we begin to identify the properties of a category and to be caught up in various ideas that the comparative process engenders, recording a memo on the emerging ideas captures these fresh theoretical musings and gives us analytic space to reflect and to work out these ideas. In this way, the act of free form memoing of thoughts, hunches and reactions to the data helps us to literally write our way to naming what we perceive in the data. This notion or writing as a way of developing thoughts is very consistent with the arguments of our colleagues in the humanities who concern themselves with understanding and teaching writing. For them, writing is a way of knowing, and it is through the process of free form writing in which various ideas and language terms are tried out that writers can come to better articulate their subject (Dowst, 1980 ; Elbow, 1981; McCrimmon, 1976). This happens, they suggest, because the act of writing makes thoughts visible and concrete, thereby allowing their authors to see what they have been thinking, to interact with the thoughts, and to modify their articulation of them (Baker, 1983; Emig, 1977; Locke and Brazelton, 1997) .

In summary, in the first stage of analytic activity, researchers engage their data. Then, through the processes of naming, comparing and memoing, we compose a set of categories and related properties that form the conceptual elements of our in-process theory. Our focus has been on the data and our conceptualization of it.

Stage 2: integrating categories and their properties

In the second form of analytic activity, as presented in the original monograph, researcher focus shifts. In this stage of analytic activity, as researchers we aim to fully develop and also to provide an organization for the conceptual categories we have been drafting. We want to make further progress in articulating our conceptual categories to the point that they can account for both similarity and variation in the exemplifying data incidents. And, we also want to make progress in formulating our conceptual scheme. To deepen development of the conceptual categories, particularly those that researchers believe are central or core, there is a slight shift in emphasis in our naming and comparing activities. For a given conceptual category, we spend less time comparing data incidents to each other and more time comparing data incidents to the drafted conceptual category, thinking about all of the elements that might make it up – its properties or dimensions. Consequently, another social loss incident in the data is now compared with the aspects of social loss that have already been identified, such as high or low loss. And, it is also scrutinized in terms of social loss more generally, to determine if this data incident points to another aspect of social loss that has not as yet been articulated.

In order to arrange our categories so that they begin to add up to a conceptual 'whole', that is a theoretical framework, as analysts we now concern ourselves with how the various conceptual elements we have composed may be arranged in relation to each other. Thus, we compare our conceptual elements in order to clarify the relationships between the categories and their properties. As researchers begin thinking about our data incidents more in terms of the whole set of categories we have under development, we will likely note possible relationships between the categories. At this stage of analytic activity, writing memos can support our efforts to articulate the significance of our categories and to begin working out on paper the relationships between the analytic elements in that framework. The form that memoing might take may also change. For example, it may be helpful to visualize the set of working categories and their possible relationships by creating simple diagrams.

Thus, the properties of high and low social loss point to a certain range in the concept of social loss. On the other hand, as previously indicated in Figure 3.2, nurses' determination of social loss may engender 'loss rationales;' both of these are related to the maintenance of professional composure. Obviously, this form of analytic activity is intended to bring some integration and organization to the conceptual categories that the previously discussed form of analysis has generated. This helps researchers to conceptualize their data into a framework that accounts for the action they observed in the research setting.

Stage 3: delimiting the theory
As categories are developed and theoretical formulations composed, analysts find themselves dealing with the third stage described, that of bounding and bringing the analysis to a close. The aim here is to settle on the framework's theoretical components and to clarify the story they have to tell about the phenomenon or social situation that was studied. Glaser and Strauss suggest that the comparative process itself works to delimit theory development at two levels: at the level of the broader theoretical framework and at the level of the theoretical categories composed from the data incidents. At the level of the framework, they argue that the theory 'solidifies, in the sense that major modifications become fewer and fewer as the analyst compares the next incidents of a category to its properties' (Glaser and Strauss, 1967: 110). Thus, the categories seem to have been developed to the point where their properties and dimensions reasonably account for the data incidents indicating that concept. At the same time, as analysts, we are able to perform a conceptual 'reduction.' By this they mean that we make a commitment to tell a particular kind of story. Thus, a decision was made to 'reduce' the social loss conceptualizing to a story about the strategies used by nurses to maintain their professional composure while taking care of patients with whose deaths varying degrees of social loss were attributed. This reducing decision, of course, in its own turn, required a return to the stage 11 form of analytic activity to ensure that the strategies that Glaser and Strauss had decided were to become the focus of the story they wanted to tell were, indeed, fully described. Thus, when we decide

on the particular story that she will tell through our conceptual framework, that decision will shape a set of choices we will make regarding what to speak in detail about and what to ignore.

A similar limiting process occurs at the level of the conceptual categories. As indicated above, when analysts integrate their theoretical categories and make a commitment to tell a particular story from their data, this reduction will help them to focus on the more relevant and robust categories. The naming and comparing activities that are central to the first form of analytic activity will, of course, result in some conceptual categories that end up being immaterial to the analytic framework and research story. Consequently, towards the end of analysis, as we work to integrate and delimit our theory and its constituent categories, we will be able to identify those immaterial categories and drop them from the framework.

Second, as we move through the analytic process, as researchers, we will have many data incidents that express our conceptual categories and their various properties. When our categories reach the point where subsequent data incidents result in no new naming activity regarding that category, its development will be complete. Other than doing a quick check on subsequent incidents to make sure that they are not saying anything new about the category, we can delimit our analysis by ignoring them. When, for example, no new dimensions of 'loss rationales' were indicated by further instances of them in the data, development of that conceptual category could stop. This is the point of *theoretical saturation*, and it means subsequent data incidents that are examined provide no new information, either in terms of refining the category or of its properties, or of its relationship to other categories.

When Glaser and Strauss describe these processes in their original monograph, all their talk of 'discovering' categories and theories and categories 'emerging' from the data can pose certain problems to novice researchers during this delimiting phase of analytic work. For example, this language invites analysts to expect that there is a theoretical reality out there in the social situation which will reveal itself. To speak in such terms almost leads to the belief that the data will choose their story, suggesting a more passive role in shaping and delimiting the research than is the case in practice. For, the practical reality is that as researchers we will have to decide on and articulate the story our data makes it possible to tell. My own experience is that after a time, analysts find that the conceptual categories we have in process are developed to the point where they are able to account pretty much for our data, and we become clear about the story. In terms of the former, this usually means that we do not exhaust every fragment and every potential category in our data. Accordingly, our theory will not be a complete account of the phenomenon we have been studying. For although our in-process framework with its constituent conceptual categories does stabilize, it cannot be considered finished. Given the understanding that theory development is emergent and processual, the theoretical framework can always be developed further. Nevertheless, a point does come in the research process where the theoretical framework is sufficiently worked out for analysts to have something substantive to say about the phenomenon they studied. We have to actively decide, though, that we have reached the point where we need to bring closure to our analysis. As researchers clarify their analytic story, it is appropriate to reintroduce into their thinking and into their memoing activity existing theoretical ideas that are relevant to the conceptual categories. This may be done by comparing the developed categories or framework with related ideas, noting areas of similarity as well as those of divergence.

In terms of the story, again, as analysts, we have to make that choice. Certainly, the decision about what story to tell, for example, about composure managing strategies, is made in light of what is most interesting in the analysis. This is clearly a determination that we make with a view to what we believe the audience for our research might be interested in.

Stage 4: writing the theory

At the fourth and final stage of the process, Glaser and Strauss describe researchers as being poised to produce a research article or monograph by virtue of possessing 'coded data, a series of memos, and a theory' (1967: 113). At stage four, the memos produced at earlier stages essentially provide the theoretical substance for the publication. The memos discussing the categories provide both the content for the categories and also a way to frame the written presentation of the theory. For example, the impact of social loss on nurses' professional composure, becomes one of the 'headings' under which the theoretical framework on social loss is presented. Finally, as the theory may well contain relationships between elements, it is fairly easy, if that be the researchers' inclination, to convert the identified relationships between categories into propositions that can be quantified using the procedures for conducting content analysis described in Chapter 2. For example, that those patients considered a high social loss will receive more attention from nurses is one potential proposition.

Constant comparison, then, is the process that supports researcher discovery of important categories, our identifying the properties of those categories and relations between categories, the extension of discovered categories to higher levels of conceptualization or abstraction, and the arrangement of those categories in relation to each other.

Selecting research situations: theoretical sampling

The previous discussion of the process of assigning meaning has hinted that in order to develop theoretical categories, researchers will likely have to engage in additional data gathering activity during their analysis. This indicates that sampling data is an issue with which researchers will need to concern themselves throughout the study, not only during the initial design stages. Those discussions also implied that the in-process analytic categories and the in-process frame in which they are arranged directly shape further sampling activity. It is in this sense of being integrated into the various forms of analytic activity that sampling in the grounded theory approach is described as being *theoretically driven*.

The logic of theoretical sampling comes from researcher commitment to developing a theory about a substantive topic, and it is this commitment to developing a theory that sets the terms for sampling throughout the study. Glaser and Strauss accordingly suggest that the practice of actively searching for and 'sampling' data in order to provide the best possible information for theorizing a substantive topic area is one of the foundational operations of this research style. Stern captures the logic of theoretical sampling, and also highlights its distinction from the random sampling that those of us trained in hypothetico-deductive methods are so accustomed to, when she makes the comment that 'selecting informants randomly makes as much sense as seeking information in the library by randomly selecting a book from a randomly selected shelf' (Glaser, 1992: xii). The rationale of theoretical sampling, then, is to direct all data gathering efforts towards gathering information that will best support development of the theoretical framework. This means that researchers enter into data collection with the supposition that it will be an open ended and flexible process that will likely be modified over the course of the study as we compose, and work to clarify, develop and refine our conceptual categories and conceptual scheme. Indeed, the logic of theoretical sampling calls upon researchers to flexibly pursue data collection to support category development to the point of theoretical saturation and the attending development of the conceptual scheme until it stabilizes. In this way, the logic of theoretical sampling gives primacy to the data because, as researchers, we cannot identify ahead of time what categories our observations will suggest are persistent or interesting, and, therefore, what we must direct our data gathering towards.

The question of what data need to be collected in order to facilitate the theorizing process is, therefore, a recurrent one. Whatever the unit of analysis, whether it be organizations, groups, individuals, situations, or particular types of event, grounded theory researchers always select them according to their theoretical relevance for the work of furthering the developing theory. This selection occurs repeatedly at many levels both during the initial set up of observations or interviews and throughout the study as analysts begin composing and relating their theoretical categories.

The logic of theoretical sampling is expressed clearly in the account Glaser and Strauss provide for how they came to study awareness of dying (1965b). In an appendix to their book of that title the theoretical concept of an 'awareness context' is given the following discovery story. (The concept of an awareness context brings into focus issues concerned with who possesses and communicates what information about the impending death of a patient.) The story begins with an account of both Glaser's and Strauss' separate personal experiences of hospitals in circumstances surrounding the death of family and friends. This, they suggest, sensitized them to concerns by patients, families and hospital staff around death expectations and who was aware of them. They then tell that they conducted a phase of preliminary fieldwork on dying in hospitals. Then, informed by their own experiences, they focused on expectations and timing of dying – identifying who knew what about the death expectations of a patient, how such knowledge affected the way staff managed a dying patient, how the organization of the hospital itself impinged on the dying patient. This initial work led to a more focused fieldwork study that examined in detail death awareness and expectations in a number of settings chosen because of the variability they would likely provide on these issues. (You will recall that my previous discussion of developing conceptual categories highlighted the concern with variation in developing multi-dimensional categories.) Glaser and Strauss describe their sampling process in this phase in the following terms:

> In our study, we began by observing on a premature baby service, intentionally minimizing the patient's awareness of dying and maximizing the expectedness of deaths (most 'premie' deaths are expected). We then observed on a cancer service, intentionally maximizing the lingering and 'nothing more to do' aspects of dying as well as several varieties of awareness of dying. In this fashion, we gradually studied various wards at different hospitals, some of them simultaneously. (1965b: 289)

As it is described in my re-telling and their narrative, the story highlights several sampling acts designed to successively focus category development and theorizing about a substantive topic. These include the following. First, the purposive selection of a research site for the phenomenon in which the investigators had an interest. Second, a preliminary phase of investigation into the phenomenon that allowed the researchers to begin creating some conceptual elements and to tentatively sketch their features. In this phase, conceptualizing on the issue of awareness and also of the likelihood and timing of death began. A third phase of investigation in which data gathering was focused on a number of situations chosen specifically because the features of awareness and the likelihood and timing of death varied considerably in them. Clearly, the premie and oncology wards provided situations in which awareness of and the likelihood and timing of death varied. And, a final phase of data gathering in various types of medically managed dying situations and in various medical organizations. This sampling strategy, therefore, pursued variation at different levels, those of the organization, the group expressed in the various departments or wards sampled, and the individual patient, in order to facilitate development of rich, multidimensional conceptual categories.

Glaser and Strauss argue that the selection of appropriate comparison groups (that is groups that are different as well as similar to ones already sampled) helps to improve the developing theory in a number of ways. Note that this aspect of grounded theory's sampling practices displays the comparative logic that is also clearly expressed in the development of conceptual categories. First, it facilitates the analytic process because the ongoing process of comparing particular features across many groups brings to researcher attention the ways in which the behaviors under scrutiny are similar and different. This helps to identify theoretical categories and to develop them more fully by, for example, discriminating the full range of the behavior under scrutiny. It is easy to see how sampling across different groups facilitated the identification of various forms of awareness context: the mutual pretense awareness context in which various parties possessed knowledge about the likelihood of and timing of death but did not reveal what they knew; the closed awareness context in which parties did not possess such knowledge; and the open awareness context in which such knowledge was understood and shared, and so on – thereby filling out the properties of the conceptual category of awareness context. Second, by examining not only comparative groups but also comparative situations, researchers may be able to determine how a conceptual category or property might be affected by different conditions; for example, what conditions affect the maintenance of a mutual pretense awareness context – the situation in which all parties act as if they do not have the information they possess? Third, sampling similar and different groups and situations ensures that researchers will collect enough information to stabilize and saturate each of the conceptual elements in their working theory. This is the point at which theoretical sampling can be brought to a close. Finally, sampling across diverse groups and situations can help researchers to discriminate the boundaries of the theory – those situations where it is more or less useful.

Theoretical sampling and the development of formal theory
Theoretical sampling, then, identifies those comparison groups that are useful to refine as well as increase the robustness of the emerging substantive theoretical framework. Also, by sampling across quite different comparison groups, analysts can develop their substantive theory into more abstract and potentially formal ones. As an illustration, Glaser and Strauss (1967) discuss how their theory of the ways in which nurses determine the social loss of a patient and accordingly vary the delivery of care can be made more formal and more abstract. By performing two

generalizations, they set the stage for developing a more formal theory. The first generalization is made with regards to the concept; the concept of social loss is raised to the more general concept of social value. The second generalization is made with regard to the actors in the situation, thus nurse–patient interaction is raised to a more general level by conceiving of it in terms of a professional service provider–client relationship. These generalizations now direct researchers to theoretically sample a number of professional–client service relationships with an eye towards discovering how the provision of service might vary according to the constructed social value of clients. These comparison groups might include a variety of different professionals, such as lawyers, accountants, therapists, etc. By using the analytic procedures previously described to develop conceptual categories, analysts will attempt to discover the underlying uniformity in the social valuing and service delivery processes that cut across all these settings. The resultant theory, then, will have greater analytic generalizability.

Similarly, Glaser and Strauss work to build a more formal theory of awareness contexts and the interaction patterns that maintain and transform them by further extending their comparative analysis beyond awareness of the dying situation to a wide range of different situations in which access to information is a central issue. Indeed, spies are offered as one relevant comparison group (1964). Interestingly, Glaser and Strauss emphasize that theoretical sampling across groups that at first glance appear to be non-comparable is a particularly useful operational practice for researchers interested in developing more general formal theory. This is a notion that Diane Vaughan appears to have taken to heart in developing her research strategy to investigate unethical behavior in organizations. As I shall discuss in Chapter 7, her comparison groups and unethical situations were the Space Shuttle accident, police misconduct and family violence .

In summary, a more formal and generally applicable theory can be developed by sampling across different substantive settings. By following this sampling strategy, researchers might develop a substantive theory of emergency organizations by gathering data across a quite different set of organizations and situations, for example, emergency rooms, fire stations, non-governmental organizations such as the Red Cross, and commercial organizations at risk for safety and industrial accidents. You may be able to think of others.

The account that I have just provided of the analytic process treats the processes of comparative analysis and theoretical sampling separately, perhaps inviting the impression that researchers sequentially focus on these processes. Such an impression would be entirely inconsistent with the research process as described in these original monographs. Composing an emerging theoretical framework from data requires that data sampling or collection and analysis should be done together as much as possible.

Evaluating the 'goodness' of the composed theory

In the substantive works about dying and the original methodological treatise, Glaser and Strauss offer a number of ways of thinking about the overall 'goodness' of the theory that researchers develop through the just described practices. In *Awareness of Dying*, they introduce two ideas and terms, specifically, 'pragmatically useful' and 'credibility' for evaluation, and they make the following statement,

> When the researchers are convinced that their analytic framework forms a systematic substantive theory, that it is a reasonably accurate statement of the matters studied, and that it is couched in a form possible for others to use if they were to go into the same field, then they are ready to publish the results. (Glaser and Strauss, 1965b: 288)

Pragmatically useful
Grounded theory acknowledges its pragmatist philosophical heritage in insisting that a good theory is one that will be practically useful in the course of daily events, not only to social scientists, but also to laymen. In a sense, a test of a good grounded theory is whether or not it works 'on the ground,' so to speak. Glaser and Strauss discuss developed theory's value as a practical guide to action through the use of four terms: 'fit,' 'understandable,' 'general' and 'control.' It must fit the situation being researched by being readily apprehensible in light of every day realities of the particular social phenomenon studied. To fit, theory and data must dovetail together. Obviously, to be useful, the theoretical framework must be understandable to people working in the kinds of social situation studied. Only then can the theory sharpen people's sensitivities to the ways in which they manage their work and the ways in which they might work differently. By being general, the theoretical framework is relevant to a number of different conditions and situations in the practice setting. Finally, the theoretical framework must provide to the person using it a degree of control over the every day situations she is likely to encounter. These criteria all highlight the close relationship between researchers' developed theory and the social situation studied. Glaser and Strauss highlighted the pragmatic relevance of their own theories. For example, they expressed the hope that nurses' clear recognition of the evaluating work that they do expressed in their theory of social loss would help nurses to avoid paying inequitable attention to different types of dying patient (Glaser and Strauss, 1964).

Credibility
Credibility in the substantive monographs and also the 1967 publication is discussed quite broadly, in terms of: the practices in which the researcher can engage during the analytic process, the rhetorical issues involved in crafting a credible publication, the relationship between the composed concepts and readers' experience, and researchers' own

beliefs. Credibility in terms of research practices, they argue, is achieved through theoretical sampling of comparison groups in order to extend the general applicability or analytic generalizability of the theory. This is achieved because, as I've discussed, the use of comparison groups simultaneously provides data for rich theoretical sampling and extends the range of conditions for which the theory is able to account. Thus, a more credible theoretical frame is one that has a greater range of analytic generalizability. While Glaser and Strauss do not address the issue, one implication of this dimension of credibility is that researchers need to collect a lot and a variety of data observations so as to allow for the comparing that creates rich and generalized conceptual categories. This issue of data density is an issue that Langley (1999) has recently underscored as important to the success of the grounded theory research process.

Credibility is also discussed as a rhetorical achievement between the author/s and their intended audience – both in terms of the qualities of the composed theoretical elements and the writing practices of the author. As far as the qualities of the composed theoretical elements are concerned, Glaser and Strauss (1965b) insist that the conceptual elements derived must not only be analytic as previously discussed, but also sensitizing. To be sensitizing, the concept must be intelligible to the work's readers in terms of their own experience. Glaser and Strauss here borrow 'sensitizing' from Herbert Blumer's ideas about the nature of social theory. As the discussion of imagery in theoretical concepts in Chapter 3 indicated, Blumer (1954) suggests that social concepts must be able to guide readers in developing a picture of the empirical instances to which they refer. Readers must be able to imagine the observations and particular situations that pointed to the theoretical categories.

Glaser and Strauss focus on achieving credibility with the readers of their research publications through writing practices that help readers to understand the theoretical framework and that produce a sufficiently vivid description of the social world studied for readers to be able to 'almost literally see and hear its people – but in relation to the theoretical framework' (Glaser and Strauss, 1965b: 290). To help readers understand the theoretical framework, they argue for deliberately building a degree of redundancy into its presentation by first foreshadowing the theory at the beginning of the manuscript, then detailing it in full in the body and finally restating it in summary form at the end. Apparently, little should be left to chance in readers' apprehending the developed theoretical scheme! To bring readers into the research setting, Glaser and Strauss suggest that authors 'show' it by incorporating into the manuscript's presentation of the theory direct quotes by informants, descriptions of the scene, and excerpts from field-note renditions of observed inter-actions. I shall have more to say about such writing issues in Chapter 7. At this point it is sufficient to underscore that Glaser and Strauss's early discussion of credibility recognize that it is not only a property of the developed theoretical frame but also a property of its interaction with its intended audience. This recognition of the rhetorical dimension of scientific writing in the 1960s predates its active consideration during the late 1970s and 1980s as part of qualitative research's moments of 'blurred genres' and 'crisis of representation.'

Finally, Glaser and Strauss also point to researchers' own subjective experience as a dimension of credibility. Specifically, they suggest that, as researchers, we need to have achieved a sense of conviction about our theorizing. They point out that this conviction comes about not only because we have been present in the setting and have systematically collected and analyzed our data, but also, because our analysis has been emergent, we have in a sense lived out our theorizing in our daily involvement in the setting.

In their substantive and methodological publications in the 1960s, Glaser and Strauss outlined the argument for developing theory from direct and close inspection of the empirical 'worlds' in which researchers have an interest. Also, they outlined the basic procedures through which researchers might compose and develop rich theoretical elements from the data observations collected from those empirical worlds. The set of basic procedures has a number of features that ensures a tight coupling between the composed theoretical elements and the research settings from which they are derived. These include: giving meaning to individual and comparative data observations, pursuing meaning expressed in the data through a flexible data gathering method that punctuates the analytic process, and holding in abeyance existing theorizing on the topic of interest until the meaning assigned to empirical observations stabilizes.

While the basic procedures and their logic are articulated clearly, there is much that the outlined procedures leave unanswered for researchers new to qualitative methods: for example, what constitutes a data fragment, how do researchers know when it is time for more data gathering, and how do analysts move past creating individual categories to the development of a conceptual framework? Indeed, bearing in mind such questions, I have often wondered how Glaser and Strauss's descriptions of the research approach were affected by their being articulated in the context of a six year study. This concern with this aspect of the context in which the approach was put to paper occurs in reference to a number of operational descriptions. For example, as I remarked in Chapter 3, I am struck when reading their research accounts by how readily their conceptualizations, especially of core categories, appeared to come to mind and to be named. This contrasts with my own experience in which the realization and naming of core categories has come late in the analytic process, and it underplays the challenge and effort involved in naming and comparing. The apparent early clarity in the conceptualizing process is also expressed in how quickly they are ready to move into theoretical sampling. This seems to me to reflect the experience and practices of researchers who have a strong sense of the particular empirical reality they are studying. This, of course, is not the case for the novice. Therefore it is not surprising that, as the originating authors began teaching the approach, and as their students and other researchers, too, began working with the approach, all worked to clarify and bring more specification to its various procedural facets. These are matters taken up in the following chapter.

5

Evolution of grounded theory

As indicated in Chapter 1, the grounded theory style of research has evolved during the three decades since the publication of the original monograph. Subsequent developments of the research practices have come from the co-originating authors, from their students, and from others within and outside of sociology who have taken up the approach and have refined or reinterpreted its procedures in applying them to their own work. Overall, the direction of subsequent methodological treatises on grounded theory has been towards further elaboration and codification in order to fill the cracks in the original monograph's articulation of the process and to capture further procedural developments in its research practices. Generally, this has increased formalization of the research practices directed towards ensuring that the conceptual elements and schemes developed through the process are sufficiently general, complex and integrated to be able to account for a wide range of variation in the phenomenon studied. Thus, much attention has been focused on procedures that facilitate achieving more general levels of category development.

In this chapter, I shall focus on the subsequent elaboration and reinterpretation of particular aspects of the set of research practices outlined in Chapter 4, and I shall do this through an examination of the methodological statements subsequently written by Anselm Strauss and Barney Glaser as well as by others who have used and commented on the approach. Furthermore, I shall highlight some of the key issues and practices that distinguish the subsequent procedural developments and that resulted in some contentious debate between the co-originators in the early 1990s. The chapter will conclude with a discussion of some of the tensions researchers face when executing this style of data analysis.

Developments in articulation of processes that support assigning meaning

In Chapter 4, I indicated that the activities of naming and comparing are basic to an analytic process that is directed towards creating a successively more general and organized theoretical account of the area of interest. Not surprisingly, developments in the articulation of the approach have sustained their focus on these practices. Particular attention, though, has been paid to clarifying procedures and to offering heuristics that help researchers to move to higher levels of generality in their conceptual categories and to bring them into organized and integrated relationship with each other, such that they add up to a conceptual framework.

In their major methodological treatises on the grounded theory style subsequent to the 1967 monograph (Glaser, 1978, 1992, 1998; Strauss, 1987; Strauss and Corbin, 1990, 1998) both original authors offer practical suggestions for creating appropriate data fragments for examination, and they both address the practices that help researchers achieve generality and integration in their theory building efforts. Both authors re-conceptualize the stages of analytic activity to underscore the achievement of increasing generality, and they both offer coding paradigms as heuristics that help the researcher to think about the nature of her overarching and integrated theoretical framing. However, these subsequent texts also express key differences in the authors' style of processing the grounded theory approach. Generally speaking, Glaser's interpretation of the necessary operational practices tends towards more openness, flexibility, and more parsimony in the elaboration of necessary analytic steps. Strauss' interpretation of the approach, on the other hand, tends towards increased prescription and formal elaboration of operational procedures. This is particularly evident in Strauss and Corbin's *Basics of Qualitative Research* (1990, 1998); these methodological texts significantly increase the technical vocabulary and prescribed operations associated with grounded theory talk and practice.

Developments in grounded theory language terms
Indeed, as if to underscore the developmental journey a good conceptual category must undergo to become analytically general, readers of subsequent monographs are struck by the proliferation of new terms associated with the activity of comparing and giving a name to data observations. And, the term that the original authors introduced to denote these two activities, namely 'code', appears in all of them. For example, the reader is introduced to: *open* coding, *axial* coding, *selective* coding, *coding* paradigms, *provisional* codes, *in vivo* codes, *theoretical* codes, and *core* codes. Admittedly, they are a bit of a mouthful. Nevertheless, they can be understood in the following way.

Open, axial, and selective coding   These terms focus attention on the slightly different aspects of naming and comparing at different levels of conceptual perspective that span the first three forms of analytic activity presented in Chapter 4. I should note, though, that while Strauss (1987) introduces all three terms to distinguish forms of naming and comparing activity, Glaser (1978) only speaks of open and selective coding. Whereas for Strauss, clarification of the process is achieved by distinguishing three stages of naming and comparing activity, Glaser (1992) argues against this, insisting that thinking about and executing these processes at two levels are sufficient. Consequently, Glaser (1978) speaks of open and selective coding, while Strauss (1987) adds axial coding, thereby describing three forms of naming and comparing activity, each with their own focus.

Coding paradigms   These are heuristic devices, templates, if you will, that support researchers' efforts to articulate the character of their theory and to place their theoretical categories in analytic relationship to each other.

Provisional, substantive, in vivo, *theoretical, and core codes*   These can all be understood as different forms of conceptual output or categories deriving from the naming and comparing process. Now, the interchangeable use of the terms code and category on the part of both originating authors tends to further complicate reading of these developments and extensions of grounded theory practice. For the sake of clarity, I will continue to refer to the practices and processes of tying data incidents to conceptual labels through their constituent activities of naming and comparing and to the conceptualized elements as categories.

Provisional categories are simply the early conceptual names assigned to data fragments. Depending on the persistence of comparable data fragments in the data set, they may or may not survive and undergo further development, turning into substantive or *in vivo*, theoretical or core categories.

As Chapter 4 indicated, when analysts settle on their core categories, they have clarified what they are building a theory of. Such categories, however, obviously come at the end of a lengthy and ambiguity-laden process of naming and comparing. Usually long before then, researchers will have been examining their data and translating their provisionally named categories into substantive or *in vivo* and theoretical categories.

Substantive or *in vivo* categories and theoretical categories (Glaser, 1978, 1992; Strauss, 1987, 1990) are the sensitizing and analytic codes that were introduced in the 1960s making a re-appearance clothed in somewhat different language. They are created, as it were, from two different resources bases. Substantive or *in vivo* categories derive from researcher examination of and immersion in the data; they capture substantive aspects of the research situation, especially the particular challenges its members face, and often they are expressed in the language of the context studied. Composure is, of course, an example. They are created through a bottom up process.

By contrast, theoretical categories tend to be broader in scope and to reflect the particular disciplinary and theoretical sensibilities of researchers. They derive from researchers' disciplinary sensibilities, and these may be sociological, anthropological, psychological or, of course, organizational; also they may derive from researchers' orienting school of thought. Theoretical categories can be thought of as being created through a kind of top down process. Thus, researchers' theoretical categories would introduce, for example, a managerial or organizational meaning to the data.

Generally speaking, analysts are more likely to create substantive or *in vivo* categories early on in the conceptualization process. Theoretical categories, on the other hand, have a higher probability of being generated a little further into coding. As my tentative language here indicates, though, these are not hard and fast rules. Also, researchers will be working with a mix of *in vivo* and theoretical categories throughout their analysis. It is not uncommon for some *in vivo* categories to be reconceptualized as theoretical ones over the course of the analytic process, while others may persist as *in vivo* within the theoretical framework.

So, in articulating these two kinds of category, as researchers, we are simultaneously working to stay very close to what is happening in our data and also to capture its relevance for our discipline. The theoretical category serves as the bridge between the context studied and the particular disciplinary context of which we as researchers are members. Maintaining the tension between *in vivo* and theoretical conceptualizing is not always easy, but it is this tension that results in a theoretical framework that is both well grounded and theoretically relevant.

Having introduced the new language terms that accompany the process of assigning meaning, let me move now to describe further developments in the operational practices of grounded theorizing.

Developments in Stage 1: comparing incidents applicable to each category

Fracturing data documents   The original monograph began its discussion of analytic practices by suggesting that researchers focus their attention on examining individual data fragments. Yet, it had little to say about just what constituted a data fragment. In subsequent works, the process by which researchers should handle their data in order to create units for analysis is made more explicit. Indeed, a preliminary procedural step and purpose is introduced that facilitates the creation of data fragments appropriate for the microscopic examination that characterizes this analytic stage. Procedurally, the recommendation is that researchers begin by breaking up the observational, interview or archival narratives that constitute their data documents into fragments for analysis. This fractures or breaks apart the data.

Fracturing their data into fragments helps researchers to step back, examine the dis-aggregated elements and conceptualize them in a way that transcends the particular interview or situation in which they were embedded. The suggestion is that the data be fractured and examined line by line (Strauss, 1987; Strauss and Corbin, 1990, 1998; Turner, 1981). Examining their data on a line by line basis helps researchers to 'get into' their data and initiate the naming activity by noting provisional names for each data fragment in the margins of their data documents. This process of fracturing the data documents into small data fragments that are each examined for meaning is the process that both Glaser and Strauss refer to through the term 'open' coding, and the names noted in the margins are provisional category terms.

The discipline of working to assign meaning on a line by line basis ensures that the data will be examined microscopically. It also precludes any tendency to assign meaning in a general way, for example, by reading over the data documents relatively quickly creating impressionistic 'themes' rather than data-specified grounded categories.

Having underscored the importance of fracturing the data documents on a line by line basis, I now need to qualify that statement to allow for some flexibility in interpreting what constitutes a line. For example, Glaser (1978) suggests that a relevant 'line' is a sentence – although in interview transcripts it is often difficult to tell just where one sentence ends and another begins. Consequently, while ensuring that they fragment their data microscopically, as Turner and his colleagues (Pidgeon et al., 1991; Turner, 1981) emphasize, researchers will nevertheless have to use their judgment as to what constitutes a piece or incident of data. So, while our data document may be technically fractured line by line, we will have to judge and to decide over and over again just what constitutes a relevant and coherent fragment. This will depend in part on our general focus, the nature of the material reflected in the data document, and, of course, on our individual perception. In some instances, a relevant fragment will be a few words, in another it might be a sentence, and in yet another, it may be several sentences (Pidgeon et al., 1991).

Figure 5.1 shows this process in a brief excerpt from a transcribed videotaped observation of a telecommuting manager making a phone call to his most senior subordinate at his company offices. Note that the excerpt from the transcript follows the recommendations Turner makes about handling the data documents (Turner, 1981, 1983). Specifically, the data document is labeled with its collection data, data source, and general topic, and the transcribed lines are numbered.

First, the beginning 9 lines of the transcribed narrative are shown, then the way in which those same lines might be fractured are presented. The fragments are of varying lengths. Each seemed to represent a meaningful and discrete event during this part of the conversation. Would you fracture in the same way, or differently? What names might you give to the fractured elements?

Both the original monograph and the originator's subsequent methodological statements seem to indicate that researchers need to maintain their data in two forms, that of the transcribed data document described

Videotape Transcript 1 (VT1)
John King
1/15/99 10:05-11 :32a.m.
[Telemanaging]

Intact Narrative:

Line

1 John: 'How's your wife? ... Oh my god, where did that come from? Mhm... pretty weird
2 (chuckles and laughs) ...her kidneys? (laughs more). Yea... did Sandy plan on doing those
3 changes in production tonight? Or, what's the plan on that? ... right ... right.. and get range
4 stuff... is that what it is? Mhmm, yea... yea. Trying to think if there's some way... well I
5 mean I can log onto production right now using this app. When we get ready to roll. And,
6 it lets me in... Oh, OK! So your concern is the old GUI. Roll out is this week or next week?
7 Is that prelim weekend, also? Well, there's something of value in a split with that but, I think
8 Edwards has to deal with it (laughs). How much more time do we have on Paul's contract, do
9 you know? What we got, about a month?

Fractured Narrative:

1–2 : 'How's your wife? ... Oh my god, where did that come from? Mhm... pretty weird (chuckles and laughs) ...her kidneys? (laughs more).

2–3   Yea... did Sandy plan on doing those changes in production tonight? Or, what's the plan on that?

3–6   Right ... right.. and get range stuff... is that what it is? Mhmm, yea... yea. Trying to think if there's some way... well I mean I can log onto production right now using this app. When we get ready to roll. And, it lets me in...

6   ...Oh, OK! So your concern is the old GUI.

6–7   Roll out is next week or this week? OK I thought it was next week?

7   Is that prelim weekend also?

7–8   Well, there's something of value in a split with that but, I think Edwards has to deal with it (laughs).

8–9   How much more time do we have on Paul's contract, do you know? What we got, about a month?

Figure 5.1   *Fracturing data into fragments for analysis*

above and in the substance of their memos. I have found it worthwhile to follow Turner's (1981, 1983) recommendation to keep a third data record, that of the concept or category 'card.' A category card essentially provides a record of categories the researcher creates, including the data incidents from which the category is abstracted. The process of physically adding each data fragment or observation to the category card forces the process of examining that data fragment with those already on the cards, and so supports and enhances the practice of comparing. Figure 5.2 illustrates the form that such a category card might take for some data fragments from the excerpted transcript just presented in Figure 5.1. It follows Turner's (1981, 1983) recommendations for keeping track of the source of the data incident, ongoing refinement of the category name, and any possible connections with other category 'cards.' (Of course, depending on ongoing comparison, the data incidents and the category name may change.) Obviously, the advent of computer

Card Number: 1	Working Label: 'Updating on Timings'
Data Source & Location:	*Data Observation:*
VT 1 John King (2–3)	Yea … did Sandy plan on doing those changes in production tonight? Or. What's the plan on that?
VT 1 John King (6–7)	Roll out is next week or this week? OK I thought it was next week?
VT 1 John King (7)	Is that prelim weekend also?
Links with:	
	Earlier Category Names:

Figure 5.2   *Example of category 'card'*

programs such as NUDIST makes automatic the work of creating such data documents.

Enhancing creativity in naming through questioning   As previously indicated, when researchers begin the process of naming data incidents their aim is to open up the data fragments to a wide range of possible interpretations – to be creative and comprehensive in articulating the different ways in which the data might be understood. Glaser uses the tantalizing phrase, 'running the data open' (1978: 56) to emphasize this aspect of opening up the data to inquiry. Thus, when researchers are urged initially to label or code a data incident in more than one way, creating multiple categories to hold it, they are constrained to think in terms of multiple possible interpretations. This process can be encouraged through the use of generative questions. And, both originating authors advocate posing questions to the data, albeit in quite different styles.

As Figure 5.3 indicates, interpretation at this and, indeed, at all levels of conceptual development is facilitated by a number of generative and neutral questions that, when used in conjunction with constant comparison, will help researchers compose interpretations that can hold the data. These questions highlight the analytic experience of trying to find a meaning that researchers can assign to the data. Even when creating

> • What is happening?
> • What is the basic problem faced by the actors here?
> • What category or what aspect of a category does this incident suggest?
> • What does this incident suggest this is a theory of (Glaser, 1978)?

Figure 5.3   *Generative questions to support conceptual naming of data*

substantive categories, the data incidents do not speak for themselves, they hint at possible interpretations which analysts try to apprehend and articulate (Schatzman and Strauss, 1973). We are always, no matter at what level of conceptual perspective, working to apprehend our data in terms of its conceptual possibilities. When these questions are used in tandem with the process of comparing data incident with data incident they can help to bring out what is stable and consistent in a working category. Further, when they are used in conjunction with the process of comparing data incident with categories, they can help researchers to sharpen and define their categories.

Strauss and Corbin (Strauss, 1987; Strauss and Corbin, 1990, 1998) take a different approach to using questions to open the data to possible interpretations. Consistent with their overall analytic style, their view of researchers are as very active, even provocative, instruments of inquiry who interrogate their data in order to arrive at their conceptualizations (Locke, 1997). In this 'interrogation,' described by Schatzman and Strauss (1973) as the idea of gaining conceptual leverage on the data, analysts look for logical thinking devices that will provide them a different perspective on their data. And, their approach to the use of questions reflects just that stance. (This is a stance to which Glaser (1992) strongly objects.) Specifically, they use questioning along the lines of who? what? why? when? how much? and so on . . . to think broadly about possible interpretations of the words or actions described in their data.

Let me provide some illustrations. In this example, analysts might use the questions to think about the meaning of a particular word or two. They might think about the words, 'how much' in the last data fragment presented in Figure 5.1, 'How much more time do we have on Paul's contract, do you know?' and ask a few questions to open up their possible meaning: What could 'how much' mean . . . When is the manager asking, 'how much' . . . Suppose the words weren't 'how much' but 'how little?' Or, to take another example, in a study examining how employees balance work and family obligations, analysts may be working with a category termed 'time to put family first.' They might more fully use logical comparative questioning like the following to gain conceptual leverage and stimulate their thinking about the category: What does it mean to decide its time? What does it mean to put family first? When does putting family first occur? When does it not occur? With whom does putting family first occur? How is putting family first achieved? What happens when someone decides its time and someone else obstructs them? Where does not putting family first occur? And so on.

Strauss and Corbin also advocate comparative thinking to open up the data. As an illustration, they discuss thinking about the word 'use' in the context of a study of drug use by comparing it with use of a computer (Strauss and Corbin, 1998). This type of comparative thinking can be traced to the sociologist E.C. Hughes, who advocated thinking comparatively about apparently incommensurate objects or terms to stimulate creative conceptualization. A better known example of such thinking is, how is a prostitute like a priest! The point is that this forces analysts to think differently about their data, and perhaps to push back on their own perceptual blinders.

As I indicated, Glaser (1992) strenuously objects to this more detailed and active provocation of the data that Strauss and Corbin (1998) denote through the term 'microanalysis.' In a text which argues that Strauss and Corbin (1990) represent a new method which he calls 'full conceptual description' and not grounded theory, Glaser takes issue with those practices of interrogating the data along various lines. Specifically, he argues that the questioning and comparative thinking are inconsistent with the grounded theory approach because they rather than the data fragments become the researchers' primary focus. In Glaser's view, the questioning and comparative thinking are 'cumbersome and over self-conscious' (1992: 60) and take researchers away from the simplicity and restraint of interpreting and comparing data in order to identify what is similar and what is different. He sees such restraint and simplicity as a central aspect of grounded theory's research practices (Locke, 1997). Nevertheless, questions like the above do provide researchers with a broader set of options that we may flexibly invoke to think widely about the possible meaning of our data. And, we will have to make our own determination of how to use questioning creatively in the context of our own experiences with the analytic process.

Composing good names for conceptual categories: fit and imagery Barry Turner, working in the domain of organization studies, adds to the clarification of practices associated with creating good category names by identifying the characteristics that should be expressed in them (1981). He points out that category names do not have to take any particular form. They can be short, fanciful or fairly long-winded. It is essential, however, that the name provide a good fit for the data incident being scrutinized, so that the particular words chosen make for a recognizable description of incidents that belong to that category.

Further, if it seems to the analysts that the fit is not satisfactory, they should make it a point to work with the category's label until this goodness of fit is achieved. The working name may be unsatisfactory for several reasons. Perhaps the terms the analysts chose originally did not quite provide a recognizable description, or perhaps the comparison of subsequent incidents placed into the category suggested a re-examination of its name, or perhaps the one category into which they were coding incidents needed to be converted into two different ones?

To push the analysts in working towards greater and greater conceptual clarity, Turner (1981, 1988) suggests another step. After several data fragments have been identified as expressing a category (from six to twelve), he recommends that analysts push themselves to write a clear formal theoretical definition of the working category label. A useful guideline in this effort is that the definition should be self-explanatory to someone uninvolved in the research process.

An example from Turner's work investigating how large scale industrial disasters occur (1978) shows the process of creating and refining category labels. A provisional category began with the following ungainly label:

> Acceptance of partial view of problem obscuring wider view. Or/confusion of one factor with another (synechdoche?) (Turner, 1981: 232)

Following more comparison and data analysis, this provisional concept evolved into a robust category of 'decoy phenomena' that pointed to one set of conditions that contribute to disasters. Its formal definition was:

> Paying attention to some well defined problem or danger distracts attention from a still dangerous but ill structured problem in the background. (Turner, 1978: 60)

Look at the second data fragment in Figure 5.1, 'Yea . . . did Sandy plan on doing those changes in production tonight? Or what's the timing on that?' A name you might marginally note for the fragment might be something like 'Updating self on timing for production changes.' It may eventually indicate a substantive category like 'Updating on timings.' Does that category name effectively portray the meaning assigned to the data fragment? What other name better captures the meaning you see in the fragment? Look now at the name that Turner generated to portray one category of conditions for large scale disaster, 'decoy phenomena.' Is the term Turner chose more vivid? Doesn't it convey more meaning than the more mundane 'updating on timings?'

Whether researchers are working on developing substantive or theoretical categories, Glaser urges them to work towards composing category names that have imagery (1978). Good imagery helps to make evident the meaning a category assigns to its data indicators. For example, in an early field study that focused on the performance of comedy in a pediatric hospital, I tried to compose names for categories that vividly portrayed the meaning I assigned to their indicating data. As an instance, I chose the name 'mastery' to denote the assurances offered to parents witnessing a set of performances enacted during the usually tense moment associated with the physical examination of their child's body. Acting as if they were 'just playing,' physicians were able to gain the cooperation of and, importantly, elicit laughter from the child, as they accomplished their medical tasks (Locke, 1996). Of course, other instances of theoretical elements with vivid imagery come to mind, including the 'garbage can' model of decision-making, and, of course, 'grounded' theory.

Developments in Stage 2: integrating categories and their properties

Transitioning from provisional to substantive or theoretical categories   As Chapter 4 indicated, in this phase of analytic activity researcher attention shifts away from the individual data fragments that she has been comparing and provisionally naming in the margins of the data documents to the more general and abstract level of the conceptual categories. However, little is said about how analysts are to make the transition between the provisional names they have recorded in those margins and the substantive and theoretical conceptual categories that now become the focus for development and integration. That conversion implies some reduction and limiting of those provisional categories.

Generally speaking, this occurs because analysts notice that many of the provisional names seem to fall into natural groupings. The grouping, of course, raises the level of generality of the working provisional categories. For example, if the brief excerpt from the transcribed video observation of John King presented in Figure 5.1 is typical, it is likely that there will be many provisional categories in the margins that relate to keeping updated on timings. These might suggest not only a more general substantive category, but also its subcategories or dimensions as various sorts of updating are delineated. For example, these might be updates on timing relative to events in the organization's annual work cycle, 'Is that prelim weekend also?' to a particular project's life cycle, 'roll out is this week or next week' or to the completion cycle of specific tasks or specific kinds of individual, 'Did Sandy plan on doing those changes in production tonight?'

In those instances when looking over the provisional categories and their names does not suggest obvious groupings, Swanson (1986b) offers this strategy. It involves the basic practices of comparing and naming, only now applied to the provisional categories. Make laundry lists of all the provisional category names. Look through them, and work to cluster them on the basis of similarities and of differences. Then, look at the clusters and see if you can name them. These will become working categories that can be further developed.

It is also useful to invoke this strategy when researchers' naming activity propagates a very large number of conceptual categories. For example, sometimes studies reported that conceptual categories numbering in the hundreds or even thousands had been generated. Both originators explicitly warn against creating and trying to work with too many conceptual categories, whether substantive, theoretical, or core (Glaser, 1978; Strauss, 1987). Indeed, they recommend that any individual study result in only one or two core categories. If the analysts are generating too many categories, they face two problems. First, it obviously requires much in the way of both personal analytic and evidenciary data resources to adequately develop a category. And, clearly there are constraints on both within the context of a doable study. Second, if researchers are developing too many categories, it is likely that they are not taking their theorizing to a sufficiently general level of interpretation to be able to parsimoniously account for a significant portion of their data. Indeed, one potential problem associated with the use of computer programs is that it is very easy to proliferate hundreds or even thousands of categories because analysts can feel 'secure' that the computer will be able to keep track of them all. But, the computer will neither be able to develop each of them fully nor to figure out how to integrate them so that they tell a coherent story.

Developing and integrating categories into a framework: axial naming and comparing and coding paradigms In 1987, Strauss introduced the term 'axial' coding to formalize the focused naming and comparing activity that was central to fully developing working categories – that is to developing their properties or subcategories and possible relationships to each other. Strauss and Corbin (1990, 1998) suggest that invoking the generative questions previously discussed, namely, who? what? where? when? why? how? and with what consequences?, are particularly useful in identifying subcategories and their possible linkages.

Coding paradigms are theoretical schemes or conceptual templates, if you will, for thinking about possible theoretical categories, how these categories might relate to each other, and what their integration might add up to. To assist in the process of bringing integration and organization to the working categories, Glaser (1978) offers some 18 families of what he calls theoretical codes or paradigms to help the researcher think analytically about and theorize the possible category integration. The coding paradigms provide ways to think about the categories and to clarify and organize what relationship each category has to other working categories. These paradigms allow researchers to flexibly consider various theoretical schemes, selecting and composing one that fits with their data.

Let me give examples of a number of these paradigms and the kind of organization and integration each offers. One is the family of '6 C's,' and it is outlined in Figure 5.4 with regard to the category, 'Updating on timings.' As Figure 5.4 indicates, using this paradigm invites integrating that substantive category within a causal-consequence theoretical framework that describes the context and conditions under which it occurs, those factors that it is contingent upon, and identifies any categories with which it may covary. Basically, researchers focus on a working category and, using the paradigm as a guide, ask themselves a series of questions examining the data in terms of each theoretical category as follows: 'Is the category a cause of another category?' 'Is it a condition, a consequence . . . etc. of another category?' (Swanson, 1986b).

It is important in identifying these possible relationships that researchers look for multiple instances of each – thus the relationships, too, have to earn their way into the framework through persistence and

Context
In what context does it occur?

Conditions
Under what conditions does it occur?
Under what conditions is it minimized/maximized?

Causes
What causes it?

UPDATING ON TIMINGS

Consequences
What are its
consequences?

Covariance
Do changes in any
category cause changes
in the other?

Contingencies
What is it contingent upon?

Figure 5.4   *The '6C' coding paradigm for the category 'Updating on timings'*

consistency, rather than being predetermined. Accordingly, there may be few instances of the 'C's' suggested by that particular paradigm in the researchers' data. Rather, it may have more to say about differences in updating activities that are expressed over time. In this case, the analysts may find a better fit with their data to invoke a process or stage model. Such a paradigm perhaps would show changes in updating behavior over time and suggest possible triggers for the movement from one stage to another. Figure 5.5 illustrates how a stage model might be compiled.

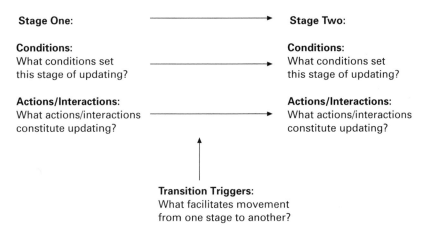

Stage One:

Conditions:
What conditions set
this stage of updating?

Actions/Interactions:
What actions/interactions
constitute updating?

Stage Two:

Conditions:
What conditions set
this stage of updating?

Actions/Interactions:
What actions/interactions
constitute updating?

Transition Triggers:
What facilitates movement
from one stage to another?

Figure 5.5   *The 'stage' coding paradigm for the category 'Updating on timings'*

Alternatively, again, the preponderance of the data may point to a broad range of ways though which updating occurs, and this may be better developed by invoking a strategy paradigm that has the analysts thinking about theorizing structural mechanisms and individual strategies. The point is that a facility with a number of coding or theoretical paradigms allows researchers to approach thinking about what their categories might add up to with a broad range of possibilities in mind. Their categories may fit one of them or they may not; however, the invocation of such paradigms will force researchers to think actively about integration possibilities.

Strauss (1987) too, advocates the use of coding paradigms as heuristics to help researchers integrate their categories. However, his work favors one paradigm – a position which Glaser finds both puzzling and worrisome (1992). The coding paradigm he articulates similarly sets conceptual categories in particular relationship to each other; however, it emphasizes action and its structural conditions. This paradigm invites researchers not only to look for those conditions under which a category such as 'Updating on timings' occurs. But, also to look for the actions and interactions that comprise and flow from it. This coding paradigm attempts to take categories and to put them in motion, so to speak. Figure 5.6 demonstrates the particular organization that this paradigm would suggest for the same category, 'Updating on timings.' As it indicates, and Strauss and Corbin's most recent methodological treatises underscore, it places a dual interest on action and interaction and the set of conditions or situational context in which it unfolds; they comment

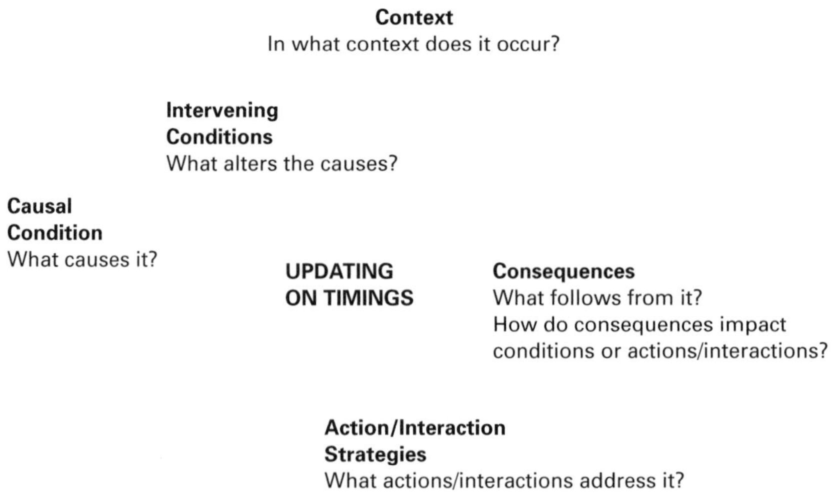

Context
In what context does it occur?

Intervening Conditions
What alters the causes?

Causal Condition
What causes it?

UPDATING ON TIMINGS

Consequences
What follows from it?
How do consequences impact conditions or actions/interactions?

Action/Interaction Strategies
What actions/interactions address it?

Figure 5.6   *The Strauss and Corbin action/conditions coding paradigm for the category 'Updating on timings'*

that 'action/interaction evolves or can change in response to shifts in the context. In turn, action/interaction can bring about changes in the context, thus becoming part of the conditions framing the next action/ interactional sequence' (1998: 165). This coding paradigm outlined for the same behavior leads researchers to be able to account for the consequences, structural conditions, interactions surrounding, and tactics for a certain action.

The point that I want to underscore here, apart from developing a robust and complex category, is that consideration of coding paradigms is a helpful move analytically to think about how we may tie together our in process analytic categories. Further, the selection of a particular coding paradigm or framework orients researchers to develop a particular type of theory around which they will orient their substantive and theoretical categories. Indeed, when Anselm Strauss's substantive and methodological work is examined over time, it demonstrates an increasing clarification of and commitment to a particular theory or way of understanding social action. Strauss' student and later his collaborator, Juliette Corbin, describes the shape of his understanding of social reality in the following terms: 'in all of his work, action is the moving organizing force of his theoretical conceptualizations and is always seen in processual terms, i.e. responding to changes in structural conditions' (Corbin, 1991: 18). This understanding, of course, strongly echoes Dewey's conception of social life as experience adapting on an ongoing basis to the problems of living (Rennie, 1998). Consequently, when we look at the coding paradigm that Strauss advocates, as compared with the '6 C's' we see more emphasis on action in its interest in strategies, tactics and interactions.

Furthermore, we see a concern with structural conditions not only at the micro level, but also at much broader social levels. This is clearly articulated in more recent methodological works (Corbin and Strauss, 1990; Strauss and Corbin, 1990, 1998) advocating that the analyst's composed grounded theories include macro structural conditions that impinge on the studied phenomena. To this end they also offer a macro coding paradigm, a 'conditional matrix' that directs the analyst to inquire into and specify the broad social, historical and economic conditions that may have a bearing on and influence the phenomenon. Clearly, this move to link micro and macro elements represents a further clarification of what a sociological theory of action should look like. In practice, however, few grounded theory studies include this conditional matrix. An interesting illustration of it, however, is available in Konecki's (1997) study of headhunting companies' recruiting efforts. Here, Konecki's conceptual scheme not only includes the micro elements, conditions, tactics, interaction, etc., but also it includes macro conditions such as the society's cultural context in explaining recruiting behavior.

It does not mean, however, that this is the only kind of theoretical model that can be developed from the grounded theory approach, because the set of analytic practices it comprises is not linked to any particular research domain or paradigm – although its adeptness at examining micro processes of behavior and interaction does express its symbolic interactionist heritage . Following the more inclusive version of theory discussed in Chapter 2 and the conception of the grounded theory approach continued by Glaser (1992, 1998), my own view is that researchers may flexibly draw on the possibilities raised by the various coding paradigms. We may compose more delimited theoretical models, for example, that include the conditions that describe when and where the action occurs, the strategies that portray how the action takes place and the consequences that identify the results of the action. Or, we may build a model about only consequences, or only conditions, if that is our focus of interest in the substantive topic. Similarly, we may build a model of strategies, in terms of individual strategies and/or strategies built into particular organizational mechanisms.

Glaser's discussion of the various coding families or paradigms as they relate to sociological interests (1978: 72–82) makes explicit the idea that numerous theoretical possibilities exist. And, for those looking for further illustrations of their use, Swanson's (1986b: 128–31) description of studies using different families or paradigms of codes provides some useful illustrations of such possibilities. For example, she describes a study that develops a type family whose conceptual subcategories include styles that capture variations of the categories detachment and involvement. Another study develops a strategy family, conceptualizing categories of behavior that can enhance relationships. Furthermore, in Glaser's view (1992), researchers serve themselves well by deliberately increasing their ability to apprehend and to draw on a broad repertoire of theoretical codes and paradigms because this will develop their ability to think theoretically, developing a coherent story from her data. Consequently, as we are developing our categories, as analysts, we need to deliberately consider possible theoretical paradigms because the form of integration they provide, whether it be strategies and tactics, conditions and consequences, and so on will shape the type of theory we are working towards.

Viewed from another perspective, selection or realization of the coding paradigm often will help analysts manage some of the ambiguity associated with building their theory. Trusting that if they work through the process, that is, if they move successively through the various analytic practices that comprise the approach, they will end up with a final integration of grounded concept demands much in the way of tolerance for uncertainty. Recognition of the kind of theoretical framework that the data and our sense making are leading to, for example, 'I am building a theory of tactics and strategies through which certain kinds of action are carried out,' can provide a kind of a theoretical anchorage (Schatzman, 1991) for analytic work of examining, gathering, and conceptualizing our data.

Developments in Stage 3: Delimiting the Theory
Chapter 4 indicated that category development and integration lead to a more limited and selective phase of naming and comparing. As the above discussion of coding paradigms indicates, single categories that have been developed in terms of dimensions or properties (subcategories) and relationships become quite large interpretive elements. In this regard, Chapter 4 also suggested that analysts will make a commitment to tell a particular kind of story from their data. This, of course, presupposes that we have made some delimiting choice about which of our categories are 'core:' that is to say, which category or categories account for the largest amount of the data, occurring most frequently and centrally, connecting or linking together a significant portion of the analytic elements. Both originating authors use the term 'selective coding' to point to the mopping up analytic activity necessary to ensure that our core categories, their subcomponents and their relationships are adequately developed and refined.

Selecting out categories   As indicated previously, when researchers make their commitment to the story they will tell, they will usually be confronted with some categories on which they have worked that simply do not fit. Should those categories be automatically dropped? Strauss and Corbin (1998) and Corbin (1986) offer a number of suggestions for dealing with this selection process that are designed to ensure that researchers do not inadvertently throw out ideas that are indeed pertinent to their theoretical framework and the story they have decided to tell through it. Strauss and Corbin (1998) recommend that researchers go through the process of diagramming out their working categories and their relationships. This visualization of the theoretical framework helps researchers to 'see' what they have integrated into their theoretical framework and to highlight those categories that do not seem to fit. Having initially identified the outliers, Corbin (1986) suggests that analysts take each outlying category and go through the following steps.

1   Check the category to see if it can be subsumed under a conceptually broader category which is part of the theory. For example, a category 'advising others' might be incorporated and subsumed under a broader existing category, 'moving information.'
2   Check to see if it is possible to collapse or combine the outlying category with one that is part of the framework by re-naming an existing category into one that is more general and with the addition of another subcategory, creating a broader category and more complex category.
3   If, however, such a broader accommodating category cannot be identified and analysts feel they have in their theory a coherent detailed and worthwhile story to tell, then at the final analytic stages,

they should drop the category. Certainly the ideas in the category might be taken up later because the conceptualization will have captured 'something.' But, at the final stage of analysis (this is not the case early on) analysts do not have to force their framework to take account of all the variation in their data.

Once researchers have worked their way through these steps such that they have settled on the categories in the framework, they need to check that each of the categories as well as their relationships have been adequately developed or saturated.

Developments in theoretical sampling

In the substantive and methodological works written in the 1960s, the notion of theoretical sampling comprises a number of ideas. These include: the idea that sampling decisions made prior to the collection of any data are informed by researchers' particular disciplinary sensibilities and by their intent to study a particular problem area; the idea that data collection is achieved through a series of doubling back steps shaped by the in process framework; and the idea that over the course of the research, theoretical sampling will result in analysts' collecting data from multiple comparison groups. Most of Glaser's and Strauss's studies have involved multiple locations. The dying studies were carried out at six different hospitals. In later methodologically oriented works, these ideas are broadened and further elaborated.

Initial data gathering strategy

Let us begin with the idea of where to start data collection. Glaser (1978) confirms that as researchers begin a study they will select individuals, groups, or settings because they believe that they will be able to provide good information on their chosen topic area. On the basis of these deliberate choices, analysts begin the process of data collection, naming and comparing, and the forming of provisional categories.

In this respect, theoretical sampling at this stage is similar to the selection process that case researchers use in selecting appropriate cases to study that were discussed in Chapter 2. Accordingly, it may make more sense to refer to these initial selection decisions as purposeful sampling. Indeed, since all sampling in qualitative research is deliberate or purposeful, Coyne (1997) suggests confusion could be minimized if the variations of sampling proposed by grounded theory were viewed as a subset of purposeful sampling. In thinking about where to gather data from initially, researchers are well served by invoking the principle of comparison. For example, researchers conducting a study of employee use of a paid time off policy may initially decide to conduct interviews with individuals based on differences on a variety of demographic characteristics. These may include: gender, whether they have young children at home, whether they have older children at home, whether they care for an elderly parent, whether they suffer from a chronic illness, whether their marital status is single or married, and so on. Such an initial sampling strategy is one bet to gather rich and varied data on the use of such a policy.

Making theoretical sampling more explicit: category development and a sampling hierarchy

The second idea, that succeeding data collection decisions should be made in terms of the analyst's working framework, is expressed by the choices that analysts make to develop the depth of their working categories. Here the purpose of theoretical sampling is to fully develop the working categories and the working theoretical framework. Thus, Glaser (1992) points out that once researchers have composed some provisional categories, theoretical sampling is expressed in their use of those categories as a basis to direct further data collection in order to better describe the categories, their properties and relationships. Invariably, the conceptualized terms of the theory will suggest a revision of researchers' original sampling strategy. For example, let us continue with the illustration studying use of the introduced paid time off policy. Suppose, that as the researchers begin interviewing and analyzing the transcripts, their provisional categories highlight the salience of the meaning and role of work in interviewee's lives and also suggest that different constructions of work identity seem to explain differences in uses and interpretations of the paid time off policy. They will, in all likelihood, compose a theoretical category named something like work identity; there will also be perhaps a substantive category accounting for differences in uses and understanding of the policy, and there will also be suggested relationships between the two. This initial work will point to a number and variety of theoretical sampling possibilities.

(i) *Sampling decisions regarding subsequent interviewees*. Whereas the researchers made their initial sampling decisions based on demographic characteristics, the variety of work identities, different understandings and suggested relationships will now shape ongoing data gathering. So, analysts will select for subsequent interviews individuals who express and vary in terms of these categories. For example, who are those people in the organization whose work strongly contributes to their definition of self, those for whom work is only marginally relevant, etc.? What are all the different ways in which the paid time off policy is used? So, researchers will look to interview people who use the policy differently, and so on.

(ii)   *Sampling decisions regarding subsequent groups.* Rather than thinking in terms of particular individuals, these categories might be developed by further data gathering from specific groups that will likely offer more information on those dimensions. For example, researchers may choose to gather more data from professionals, managers and hourly employees. And, indeed, the analysts may choose to pursue these groupings in other organizations, extending the number of sites involved in their study.

(iii) *Sampling decisions regarding the structure of data gathering.* In addition to influencing whom they gather data from, the analysts' working framework will also likely suggest that they ought to amend their data gathering mechanisms, namely their interview questions or observations, so that they can gather more information about the issues reflected in the categories. For example, questions that explore how interviewees think about themselves in relation to their work should be added to the interview protocol.

(iv)   *Sampling decisions regarding the existing data set.* In the originators' discussion of theoretical sampling, they imply that theoretical sampling always proceeds in terms of new information that researchers gather as they proceed with their analysis. A strong case can be made, however, for theoretical sampling within the existing data set. That is, the researchers re-examine their transcribed interviews with the working categories in mind, ensuring that they have captured in those working categories all the information that they have to offer. In my experience, this form of doubling back will occur several times over the course of analysis. For, even though the analysts have fractured and created category names for their field notes or interview transcripts, as Hawk (1991) points out, the researchers will find information in their documents whose significance went unnoticed. For example, they may notice that a phrase that was part of a larger data fragment might, in fact, be separately interpreted.

There are various ways, then, in which theoretical sampling may shape subsequent data collection. While it may well mean that analysts add to the study subjects or groups or organizations that they had not initially considered nor approached, this is not always the case. Strauss (1987) clarifies that this searching may be accommodated by the researchers' existing data pool, for example, a single organization that constitutes the site for the study. Nevertheless, data collection will be affected by initial conceptualizing. For example, even if researchers' original slate of interviewees is sufficiently broad to allow them to fully develop the categories in their framework, they will still modify the original interview questions so that the working conceptualizations can be better developed. Accordingly, if researchers are conducting observations or are analyzing organizational documents, they can similarly expect to modify their strategy for conducting observations or their examination of organizational documents in order to better focus ongoing data gathering in terms of the in process categories.

To help in making sampling strategies more explicit, Strauss and Corbin (1990, 1998) offer a three-leveled sampling hierarchy that dovetails with their articulation of varieties of naming and comparing. It is consistent with their overall increase in codification and formalization of practices associated with the grounded theory research approach. The variety of theoretical sampling strategies described in Table 5.1 clearly underscore the doubling-back aspect of data gathering in the grounded theory approach, demonstrating how data gathering is integral throughout the analytic process.

It should be noted that Glaser (1992) takes issue with Strauss and Corbin's (1990, 1998) codification of sampling strategies, arguing two points. First, it provides more technical language and prescriptions for researchers to assimilate, thereby making it more difficult for them to apprehend the basic logic of theoretical sampling, and second, that it introduces a degree of rigidity into the research process that is inconsistent with grounded theory's flexible ethos. I tend to agree that proliferation of grounded theory 'jargon' can be a bit much for the reader. Also, I believe that that the hierarchy of sampling strategies attendant on a hierarchy of coding practices can invite potential researchers to expect a linearity in their analytic work that their experience will not bear out. At the same time, however, the basic idea that as researchers conceptualize their data at higher and higher levels of abstraction they should work to ensure that each conceptualization and its relationships are as fully developed and described as possible bears

Table 5.1   *Strauss and Corbin's (1990, 1998) theoretical sampling strategies*

Naming and comparing practice	Theoretical sampling strategy
Open	*Open sampling* – relatively indiscriminate sampling of those existing and new persons, places and situations that will provide the best opportunities for collecting relevant data
Axial	*Variational and relational sampling* – focused sampling of those existing and new persons, places and situations that will provide opportunities to gather data about the properties and dimensions of the categories as well as how the categories are related to each other. Data gathering in terms of the coding paradigm is also clearly implicated here
Selective	*Discriminate sampling* – very focused and deliberate sampling of those existing and new persons, places and situations that will fill in and refine the core categories' story line and the proposed relationships between categories

reinforcing. This, of course, is captured in the idea of theoretical satura-tion – analysts can find no new information about the category or its relationships.

Treatment of negative cases

A key issue that arises in theoretical sampling involves analysts' treat-ment of so-called negative data incidents, that is, an incident which contradicts some aspect of the emerging framework. Suppose, for exam-ple, that analysis has indicated that a work identity that is central to a person's sense of self results in very conservative use of the paid time off policy. Suppose, further, that the analysts now come across an instance where an individual whose work identity seems to be central to how she/he describes her/himself does not use the policy conservatively. What do they do? Does such an instance negate the relationship between work identity and interpretation of the paid time off policy that they have elaborated?

In the logic of theoretical sampling, the instance of a negative case does not discredit the working framework. Rather, it indicates that the framework is not developed to the point where it accounts for sufficient complexity in the phenomenon. The negative case, therefore, provides an opportunity for exploring and articulating more complexity in the researchers' in process theory. The researchers will have to identify the conditions in which that relationship does not hold. And, to do this, they will likely have to pursue additional data gathering to investigate it. The negative instance, consequently, is an occasion for further theoretical sampling because by looking for other such instances, analysts will be able to modify their theoretical scheme in order to be able to account for it. Indeed, researchers are encouraged to look for negative instances because they can help to develop more sophisticated and complex theoretical frameworks.

Tensions involved in carrying out the grounded theory approach

Consideration of the grounded theory approach has underscored the active and central role played by researchers in assigning meaning, an issue that the originators address in the concluding pages of the original monograph. As analysts, we are the primary instrument for conceptual-izing and generating theory, and the burden of naming and bringing into existence some process or concept falls squarely on our shoulders. That said, the practices outlined in Chapters 4 and 5 will inevitably result in researchers experiencing a number of tensions as they work to interpret and meaningfully conceptualize their data. These tensions associated with the process of assigning meaning are expressed in a number of apparent contradictions. These are: contradictions between immersing themselves totally in the data in order to assimilate it into their thinking and getting sufficient perspective on their thinking in order to be able to fully articulate thoughts and to critically examine their analysis; contradictions between creating names that stay close to the data to achieve goodness of fit and creating names that creatively abstract from the data to achieve a high level of generality; and, contradictions between holding in abeyance existing theoretical frameworks so that they do not foreclose potential interpretations and drawing on and cultivating theoretical sensitivity in order to compose categories and a theoretical scheme. To a degree, these tensions highlight the importance of analysts being able to contend with and move back and forth between both the subjective and the objective aspects of the analytic process. These are represented in Figure 5.7, and each is given further discussion below.

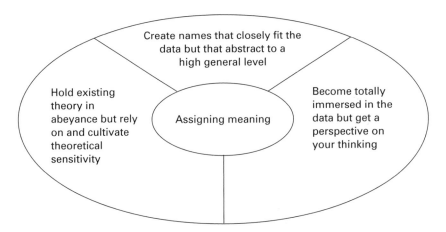

Figure 5.7   *Tensions experienced by the researcher working to assign meaning*

Total immersion in the data and gaining perspective on thinking

In various ways, researchers are encouraged to immerse themselves in the data. This is so that they can absorb it, being able to recall numerous data fragments, and so that such fragments and their thoughts about naming can enter day to day thinking and especially their out-of-awareness processing. Certainly, the purpose of researchers' initial naming and comparing activity is to fracture their data documents and to begin formulation of some initial categories. However, it also forces analysts to spend time attending to their data – getting it in to them – so that they can 'work' with it. Concepts, ideas about concepts and excerpts from data noticeably occupy their thinking, conscious and otherwise. Interestingly, William Foote Whyte's (1991) comments on how ideas about his data come to him seem to underscore the importance of allowing for some out-of-awareness processing of data that has 'entered' the researcher. He notes that 'some of my best ideas emerge out of my unconscious or semiconscious mind, when I am not at my desk but out weeding the garden or doing some other unrelated activity' (Whyte, 1991: 270). Indeed, such immersion in which researchers become almost subject to their data is one of the characteristics of the analytic process. Glaser, for instance, discusses the 'drugless trip' (1978: 24), a phase in the analytic process that often follows an extended period of 'data input' through systematic line by line naming. In this phase, analysts' thinking about the data overcome them, and they are flooded with ideas about it and about their study.

Certainly, the practice of memoing, which should be triggered by this experience, helps researchers to capture such thinking. However, the question of whether such thinking will stand up to reconciliation with the data and whether it will advance development of categories and the theoretical framework is deferred; that will be determined by the data. While memoing does much in the way of capturing thinking to make it available for subsequent careful scrutiny, it is useful for researchers to be able to talk through the thinking captured in the memo with others, in order to check if their thinking holds up to scrutiny by another and in order to explore the potential implications of such thoughts for the theoretical scheme.

Besides checking on whether our thinking and category development make sense, talking about our work to someone else can help us to get a perspective on the direction our analysis seems to be taking, because it literally allows us to 'hear' what we are thinking and also because that outsider may be able to identify a pattern in our thinking by reflecting back what she hears. For instance, during our analysis of the ways in which journal articles create opportunities for contribution, there was period of time in which my colleague, Karen Golden-Biddle had to be out of town; I worked in a data intensive way for about ten days on the ongoing development of categories while Karen, temporarily detached from the data, was reading broadly to stimulate theoretical thinking about our work. I recall the telephone call we scheduled shortly after her return in which we spoke about the categories. While we felt comfortable that we had a number of categories that were well on their way to being saturated, we had been having difficulty stabilizing what they all added up to. I had an idea that the categories pointed to a particular process that had something to say about how opportunities for contribution were created, textually, but I was unable to integrate all of the categories around it. They simply wouldn't fit together. After a time, Karen interrupted my going on and on about the categories, data, and what it might all mean, claiming: 'That's it!' Stopped dead in my tracks, and clueless, my response was: 'What's "it"'? She continued, offering that what she had heard me saying and describing through the data fragments made sense (in light of some reading she had been doing on literary writing) if we thought not of one, but of two overlapping processes. When we talked though the categories and data fragments in light of two potential processes, the framework stabilized, and the remaining necessary theoretical sampling and category development became clear. These two processes, constructing intertextual coherence and problematizing, eventually became the core categories for our framework for the construction of opportunities for contribution. Ironically, an early memo that we had discussed contained a reference to 'two processes,' but at the time it was written neither she or I appreciated its implications. My colleague's temporary time away from the project allowed her to gain some distance from the naming activity in which I was immersed, enabling her to bring a fresh perspective and see a 'forest' while I was very much tangled up in its 'trees.'

Obviously, managing the tension between total immersion and analytic perspective or distance implies that researchers should parse their analytic time in a such a way as to create periods of total immersion in analytic activity working alone alternated with periods of external discussion and examination working with others. And, many researchers involved in theory development, including Glaser (1978), Turner (1981, 1983), Vaughan (1983), Strauss (1987), Strauss and Corbin (1990, 1998), and Star (1991), underscore the importance of involving outsiders in discussions about the analysis. This can be through the use of a formal, regularly scheduled research group or seminar discussion or by less formal means, for example, by recruiting others to make themselves available to read, listen and respond to researcher thinking.

Staying close to the text and formulating high order, general interpretations
As our discussion of the naming process indicates, researchers need to stay close to the data represented in the fractured data documents in order to ensure that their naming demonstrates a good fit to the data. And, the expectation that they will be formulating a number of substantive or *in vivo* categories reinforces this understanding that they will be creating categories that closely reflect what is potentially expressed in the data documents. On the other hand, that same discussion also indicated that researchers need to conceptualize and name categories at a sufficient level of generality to be able to account for numerous and varied fragments.

As Rennie (1998) points out, when researchers work with small circumscribed units of meaning or 'names,' diligently staying close to the denotative meaning of the text, they can easily find themselves confronted with two problems. First, their categories may do little more that repeat the text of the data document. As such these will tend to be very concrete and to offer little insight into what may be happening in the situation they are studying. Second, researchers can easily fall prey to developing a huge number of categories. As already indicated, working with a very large number of conceptual categories, in the hundreds or thousands, is more than a person's analytic resources will allow.

The counter measure to these outcomes is achieved when researchers tend, on the whole, towards achieving abstraction in the naming process but always reconcile those abstractions with their data fragments. However, as researchers move to a more general and abstract form of naming, more demands are placed on their creative resources in interpreting and naming their data (Rennie, 1998). The creative pursuit of naming requires researchers to move back and forth between two poles: at the one pole, exploring what is imaginatively and poetically evoked by the text inscribed in their data documents and at the other pole, confronting the concrete language terms of the text. Mintzberg (1979) discusses the centrality of the creative leap in the theory building process where researchers have to attempt to generalize beyond their data. My image of this process is of analysts 'jumping away' from the text in an imaginative move that creates a possible understanding of what might be happening in one or more data fragments, and then of their being 'pulled back' by the specific and material language terms in the data. They have something when, having 'been pulled back,' their imaginative conceptualization is congruent with their data fragments. In my own work, these two moves have come to be respectively elicited by the neutral questions Glaser (1978) proposes that researchers use to inquire into their data. Specifically, the question, 'what is happening?' tends to occasion the imaginative and poetic move pushing researchers to try for inventive responses. On the other hand, the question, 'what category or aspect of a category does this incident suggest?' tends to confront them with the limits on thinking set by the language terms of the text. In the study of contribution just discussed, one of these imaginative 'jumps' brought to mind an image of a jigsaw puzzle in which the same pieces could be reshaped and fitted together to create very different 'pictures' of the literature. That image was eventually articulated in the name 'intertextual coherence,' which highlighted how existing works are shaped into one of three possible representations of the state of understanding about a phenomenon.

Rennie, working within the clinical domain of psychotherapy, captures the tension inherent in the naming process in the following terms that highlight the to-and-fro movement in terms of subjective and objective poles of researcher experience.

Within this creative process, grounded theory analysts work with their own experience when attempting to understand the experience of others mediated through the text. It is within the interplay between external and internal experience that the art of good interpretation lies. Too much caution expressed as reluctance to give vein to subjectivity can result in 'missing' the life of the experience under study. Alternatively, giving too much reign to subjectivity expresses the life of the analyst more than that of the respondents. Good interpretation thus involves living inside and outside the experience while monitoring of the degree of fit between the two aspects. (1998: 11)

It is in the creative mode that researchers can generate interesting category names that are vivid and have grab, and, of course, can account for a significant number and variety of data incidents.

Bracketing out theory and drawing on and cultivating theoretical sensitivity

I have earlier characterized the grounded theory approach as exhibiting a conservative stance towards extant theory. This is expressed in the passionate general denunciation of grand theory that is presented throughout *The Discovery of Grounded Theory* and in the specific injunction that researchers should, as they attend to the analysis of their data, temporarily suspend from thinking all preconceived notions, expectations and previous theorizing related to the substantive area they are studying. So, researchers do not introduce to their analysis specific concepts or propositions and, when these do come to mind as analysts name and compare their data fragments, they temporarily bracket them out.

At the same time, however, researchers are told that they have to be sufficiently 'theoretically sensitive' in order to be able to conceptualize their data (Glaser and Strauss, 1967: 46). They emphasize that 'the root sources of all significant theorizing is the sensitive insights of the observer, himself' (1967: 252). And, Glaser (1978) underscored the importance of such theoretical awareness when he chose that phrase to title his second monograph on the grounded theory approach. The notion of theoretical sensitivity, it seems to me, rests on the premise that researchers cannot apprehend something unless they are equipped with a perceptual apparatus, including language terms, that allows them to discern and pay attention to it: an apparatus that is sensitive to it. Researchers' ability to apprehend their data derives from a number of sources. These certainly include disciplinary training and, perhaps, commitment to a particular school of thought such as symbolic interactionism, or to a particular paradigm of inquiry, be it modernism, interpretivism or postmodernism. These sources of theoretical sensitivity orient researchers to particular features of the setting and the phenomenon they are studying, and they provide a perspective from which the analysts may compose their theoretical insights. Also, as our discussion of coding paradigms indicated, they provide them with ways of thinking that can be tried out and adapted in light of the data.

Theoretical sensitivity, also, can be derived from sources outside of the researchers' disciplinary domain, for example, from personal experiences outside the research situation, and from the experiences of others, to include those experiences articulated in novels or any other means by which an individual experiences the world. The account that Glaser and Strauss provide of their sampling procedures for developing the concept of awareness contexts clearly demonstrates the way in which both their personal experiences with the very phenomenon they were studying –

their naïve field experience – helped to spark insights that informed theory development. In the appendix to the awareness context monograph (Glaser and Strauss, 1965b), Strauss' personal experience is narrated as helping him to identify and see as problematic the issue of awareness, while Glaser's experience is narrated as offering insights about the relationship between death expectation and the way that the ward staff dealt with the dying patient and family members. But, then, they were able to link personal and professional domains, discerning the sociological implications of what they had experienced. Similarly, to take an example from the management realm, in analyzing data about an organizational newcomer's mentoring experience, researchers could recall all their own newcomer experience in different kinds of organization and use them in a comparative way to help think about what their data might mean. Parallel personal experiences, thus, may be a source of theoretical insight.

The prominent evolutionary theorist, Stephen Jay Gould (1993) offers an interesting account of his source of insight for the argument he constructed in his controversial and much cited paper 'The spandrels of San Marco and the Panglossian paradigm: A critique of the adaptationist programme' (co-authored with Richard Lewontin). This was an invited address, delivered at The Royal Society, London, and published in their *Proceedings*. He describes how he came upon what he refers to as the 'most unconventional and probably most successful aspect' (Gould, 1993: 323) of the paper, its metaphoric use of an architectural element, the spandrels of San Marco cathedral. He begins this 'insight story' by noting that three months prior to having to deliver the address, he had visited Venice for the first time, then he continues as follows.

'I had been thinking about adaptation for I knew I had to prepare for the London talk. These things can only happen once or twice in an intellectual lifetime, but I had an epiphany of sorts, appropriately enough under the great dome of San Marco. I looked up at the spandrels, worked out the complex (and lovely) iconography of four evangelists above me personifying the four biblical rivers, and the whole argument hit me all at once – a strange feeling of almost manic exhilaration followed by the total calm of understanding . . .'

While Gould is here referring to the construction of an argument, rather than the conceptualization of empirical data, his account, nevertheless, highlights how an experience he had in one personal context became a source of insight, and indeed a way to conceptualize and frame his argument against the adaptationist project in evolutionary biology. The point is that analysts can 'sample' across a wide range of possible sources to generate many ideas that might potentially give shape to their thoughts about what might be theoretically possible in their data. But, these then have to be held in tension with what researchers are encountering in the field situation. Appropriately, Glaser and Strauss (1967) highlight the importance to each researcher of finding a way of stimulating insight from sources outside as well as inside the field that works best for them. For some, this may mean holding in abeyance all reading while they are actively engaged in the field; for others, this may mean reading quite different material, for example, novels or biographies or related topics in quite different disciplines. All these materials are read to provide different stimuli for thinking. For others, it may mean reading on related topics in different disciplines, while for others still, it may mean periodically sampling their discipline's literature as the field work progresses. Whatever style researchers arrive at for helping them to think creatively about what is happening, as always, insights generated must be worked out in relation to the data. That is, they must be transformable into categories, properties, and proposed relations.

Part Three

The Grounded Theory Approach in Management and Organization Studies

---
6

Bringing grounded theory to studies of management and organizations

In Part Three, I move more fully into examining the grounded theory approach in management and organization studies, paying attention to what happened to this style of qualitative research when used in studies in this domain. This part of the book will also examine how grounded theories as written accomplishments have been composed and represented in management and organization journals.

By the 1970s, the grounded theory approach had been taken up and used in studies of management and organization behavior that were being published in prominent journals. As noted, it has been one of, if not the most, prevalent methodological citations appearing in qualitative studies published in this discipline. Over the same time period, discussion of qualitative approaches became visible in management and organization journals. For example, in the United States in 1979, *Administrative Science Quarterly* published a special issue devoted to discussion of strategies and issues in conducting qualitative research and in 1983, the *Journal of Management Studies* did the same in Europe.

Over this 30-year time period, the grounded theory approach and its associated practices have been taken up in different ways. The approach was adopted as the organizing procedural frame for their work by a number of researchers pursuing the qualitative study of organizations. Other qualitative researchers have flexibly and selectively adapted its practices, creating variations of grounded theorizing by drawing on other methodologically oriented resources. As interest in qualitative research grew, many other texts (largely based in other disciplines) offering procedural guidance to researchers interested in pursuing qualitative research were also published, and some of these have made their way into management and organization studies where their presence and influence are apparent. Interestingly, it appears that for several of those researchers who have been drawn to the grounded theory style of qualitative research, two other procedural guides that strongly express the modernist paradigm have been taken up. First published in 1984, they are *Qualitative Data Analysis* (Miles and Huberman, 1984, 1994) and *Case Study Research* (Yin, 1984, 1994). Other guides to qualitative data analysis that appeared in roughly the same time frame, for example, *Learning From the Field* (Whyte, 1984), and, of course, Glaser's (1978) *Theoretical Sensitivity* are less visible. In the mid 1980s (prior to publication of Strauss's subsequent methodological works), a number of researchers who chose to pursue theory building studies in the United States turned to the proceduralized qualitative research accounts offered by Miles and Huberman (1984) and Yin (1984). They combined these with their own resources to develop workable approaches to conducting qualitatively oriented theory building studies. Of course, as these researchers networked and, as their studies began to appear in prominent journals, their approaches served as models that other researchers took up and incorporated into their own studies.

Chapter 6 starts by considering the compatibility of the grounded theory approach with the research interests and commitments of management and organization scholars. I then look into how we have adopted as well as adapted it, highlighting the kinds of grounded theory that researchers have developed. The final section of this chapter examines whether the study of management and formal organizations, specifically the issue of access, poses any constraints on the approach.

To accomplish this task, I drew on a number of resources: published empirical studies that draw on the grounded theory approach; published methodological discussion of the approach and its practices; conversations with other researchers who have relied on the approach in their own work; and, of course, my own experience. The ideas I discuss were arrived at by following the general contours of the grounded theory approach – that is I closely 'read' the different resources; I then built categories regarding the use of the grounded theory approach by naming what the data resources suggested and comparing those named suggestions across other data resources. Similarities reinforced existing categories while differences suggested new categories or variations on already identified ones. I gathered additional resources to fill out categories, for example, looking for more studies that combined different orienting theoretical perspectives with grounded theory's analytic logic and practices. Finally, those categories were integrated into the larger categories – compatibility, adoption and adaptation – presented next.

Compatibility of the grounded theory approach: its suitability

As a general statement, much of the theoretical concern in management and organizational studies is with substantive topics such as decision-making, socialization, and change. Grounded theory is particularly useful for examining those situated processes. Furthermore, our domain is also much concerned with issues associated with individual and group behavior (albeit behavior embedded in the vertical and horizontal structure of formal organizations) – again a research locus in which grounded theory with its interactionist heritage is particularly useful (Glaser, 1992). This general match between an analytic approach and management and organization studies should come as no surprise. After all, its genesis, in no small part, lay in studies of professional work carried out in complex organizational settings. That said, a number of scholars have argued that grounded theory is particularly appropriate to researching managerial and organizational behavior for a number of reasons.

Capturing complexity
The grounded theory style adapts well to capturing complexities of the context in which action unfolds, enabling researchers to better understand all that may be involved in a particular substantive issue. Martin and Turner (1986) contend that the grounded theory approach is well suited to the study of complex entities because of its ability to produce a multifaceted account of organizational action in context. More recently, Orlikowski advocated and pursued a grounded theory approach to better understand organizations' adoption and use of CASE (computer aided software engineering) tools because it would allow her as a researcher to capture more of the complexity involved in adopting this and other technological tools. Specifically, it would allow her to focus on the contextual and processual elements of adoption and use as well as on the actions of key players associated with this technology-based change. By contrast, she characterized prior research as focusing on 'discrete outcomes, such as productivity, systems quality, and development costs, while neglecting the intentions and actions of key players, the process by which CASE tools are adopted and used, and the organizational context within which such events occur' (1993: 309).

Linking well to practice
The concern with substantive issues and the ensuing theoretical accounts that this approach generates have proved especially useful to help organizational members gain a perspective on their own work situations. As Chapter 4 indicated, Glaser and Strauss (1964) believed that helping nurses to recognize how they socially evaluated patients would help them deliver better care. Turner shares their conviction, explaining that because these theoretical accounts 'conform closely to the situations' researchers study, they are 'likely to be intelligible to and usable by those

in the situations observed' (1983: 334). This form of theorizing then, with its insistence on pragmatic usefulness as a criterion of good theory, is particularly adept at bridging theory and practice, providing employees and managers a way to identify and institute changes that might improve their situations.

Partington (2000) echoes this sentiment, contending that the grounded theory approach is in two respects well suited to the aims of contemporary mode 2 management research. (Mode 2 research shows concern for the gap between the academy and practice domains, advocating research aimed at advancing the interests of the latter.) Specifically, mode 2 management research is trans-disciplinary, and as such it is less likely to bring with it mature theoretical frameworks developed within the boundaries of particular academic disciplines. Furthermore, it underscores the importance of accessing the tacit knowledge of organizational actors. Thus, Partington (2000) recommends and has used the approach to develop a grounded normative model that accounts for the actions of managers seeking to implement planned organizational change initiatives.

Supporting theorizing of 'new' substantive areas
The naturalistically oriented data collection methods as well as the approach's theory-building orientation permit the investigation and theoretical development of new substantive areas as they 'arrive' on the organizational scene. For example, many of the features of managerial and organizational life associated with the revolutionary effects of technology are an obvious instance of such 'new' areas of concern. Eisenhardt and her colleagues have accordingly adopted a grounded theory building approach to study features of life in so-called high technology organizations. The nature of strategic decision-making in fast paced environments (Eisenhardt, 1989a; Eisenhardt and Bourgeois, 1988) and the organizational capacity to achieve continuous change (Brown and Eisenhardt, 1997) are two instances of substantive theorizing about the nature of life in such organizations.

Similarly, in the early 1980s as plant closings and downsizing appeared as a feature of managerial and organizational life, Sutton and his colleagues used such an approach to develop theory about death and decline as a feature of organizational and managerial life. These included studies of processes associated with organizational death (Harris and Sutton, 1986; Sutton, 1987) and also the management of the social stigma associated with organizational decline and bankruptcy (Sutton and Callahan, 1987). As a final illustration, the past decade and a half has witnessed ever increasing globalization and the development of associated comparatively new organizational forms. One of these is the international joint venture; this organizational form, too, has been the subject of grounded theory building research. For example, it has been used to develop theories of managerial control (Yan and Gray, 1994) and theories of alliance-based knowledge transfer in such organizational forms (Inkpen and Dinur, 1998).

Enlivening mature theorizing
The grounded theory building approach has been used to bring a new perspective and new theorizing to mature established theoretical areas, enlivening and modifying existing theoretical frameworks. For example, Gersick describes how she pursued this approach when during a study of group effectiveness, the group's behavior did not conform to existing theoretical models of group development. This prompted her to 'choose an inductive qualitative approach to increase the chances of discovering the unanticipated and to permit analysis of change and development in the specific content of each team's work' (1988: 12). The punctuated equilibrium model of group development that focused on previously unaddressed issues of timing and transition in group life resulted from this work.

A further illustration of this point is evident in the area of leadership, perhaps one of the most heavily theorized subjects in management and organization studies. Recently, contending that a strong psychological orientation has dominated leadership theorizing, Parry (1998) has argued that leadership needs to be researched as a social process rather than through the study of the person of the leader, especially those persons who occupy senior and formal leadership roles in the organization. He claims that leadership should be conceived as one of Glaser's (1978) basic social processes and, following the tenets of theoretical sampling, theories of leadership should be developed from examination of leadership incidents in a variety of different organizational contexts and at various levels of hierarchy. Such theoretical development would refresh and significantly complement existing theorizing on the topic. It is also worth noting that Eisenhardt's studies focusing on high velocity or fast paced environments (described above) brought a new substantive context and a fresh perspective to the well worn theoretical ground of organizational decision-making.

A different angle to the notion of enlivening mature theoretical perspectives is that use of a grounded theory approach can make sure that our theories stay current with the organizational realities they purport to explain. In this vein, Singh (1999) explained in a personal communication that, had she not started her research 'bottom up' (that is with the data incidents and what they suggested rather than with existing theory) in her study of commitment, she would have ended up excluding much of her findings. Instead, by adopting a grounded theory building approach, she was able to develop a model that demonstrated how in practice settings, the concept of commitment had moved on, away from the theoretical schemes that are still in place in the academy. The issue of updating and ensuring that theoretical frames are contemporary with the changes that have occurred in today's workplace is an intriguing and provocative one. For instance, it has been some 30 years since Mintzberg (1973) conducted his landmark studies of managerial work. Since that time, our work organizations have been subject to several waves of change. Has the function of management shifted in any way? Is it not time to revisit our understanding of the managerial function in a way that would allow us to conceptualize it differently, to identify those aspects of management that might have been left behind, to reinterpret aspects of the work that have changed, and to capture any new areas of managerial attention and concern?

Adoption of the grounded theory approach

Early adoption

As indicated, qualitative studies in which researchers adopted grounded theory's investigative logic and its basic operational practices as a whole, so to speak, began to appear in the then newly established discipline of organizational behavior in the early 1970s. The earliest study that I could find published in a journal in our domain appeared in 1971. Hobbs and Anderson (1971) adopted the approach to conceptualize how academic departments operate based on the behavior of department personnel. Over the course of the study, the authors interviewed members of 34 academic departments in five colleges using semi-structured interview schedules. Department types (social sciences, humanities, natural sciences, life sciences, and professional) as well as institution types (state universities, state colleges, and church related colleges) were varied in their sample. The description of their analytic procedures suggests that they closely conformed to the practices associated with constant comparison and theoretical sampling. They specify that,

> '. . . categories of topics which constituted departmental concerns were constructed from the data gathered in initial interviews; additional data were then collected to permit amendment – including occasional deletion – and the integration of those categories. Finally, the refined categories were embellished by explanatory categories, also grounded in the data, until the model of the organization of academic departments emerged' (1971: B-135).

Their theory summarizes how different structures of authority, accountability and power relate to various tasks and problems department personnel confront.

The work of Barry Turner is included in these early grounded theory studies, and in many respects his work models (as discussed in Chapter 5) and even extends the application of grounded theory's analytic procedures. Furthermore, it serves as an exemplar of the kind of insightful, fine grained, and pragmatically useful theorizing that researchers working in this style can achieve.

For example, a study carried out from a socio-technical theoretical perspective investigated the relationship between a firm's production system and its social system in batch production factories (Reeves and Turner, 1972). This was a field based study in which researchers gathered data from observations and interviews with managers and supervisors in three organizations. Two of the organizations were batch production factories; later (consistent with the principle of theoretical sampling), data from a third organization, a mass production factory were added. Categories were developed from the field based data and were composed into a theoretical model that explains how managers and supervisors dealt with the complexity and variability associated with batch production.

Turner's (1976) fine study of the conditions under which failures of organizational foresight contribute to the incidence of large scale disasters similarly follows the contours of the grounded theory approach. Instead of employing a field-based study, however, Turner relied on the detailed accounts of action available in the public inquiry records of three disasters from which to constitute his data documents. The disasters included: the slide of a portion of a colliery tip onto the Welsh village of Aberfan killing close to 150 people, most of whom were children whose school was engulfed by the coal; a collision between a slow moving transporter and an express train as the former negotiated an automatically controlled railroad crossing; and a fire in a holiday leisure center. These incidents were sampled because they provided different instances of serious disasters, yet they had in common the informational complexities associated with failures of foresight.

Interested in the issue of information complexity, Turner took detailed notes of the contents of three disaster inquiry reports, and these constituted his data documents. These notes were then fractured into data incidents that were named and composed into conceptual categories. In this way, Turner was able to identify common features associated with the development of all three disasters, and to compose a model that cataloged and detailed the conditions under which the kinds of foresight failures that led to disastrous consequences could occur.

These early studies demonstrate full adoption in several respects. Theoretical sampling is evident in choice for variety in research sites, in the narrowing and refocusing of information seeking, and in the addition of research sites. Furthermore, as Turner (1976) tells the story, the disaster study itself represents ongoing theoretical sampling from the batch production investigation. According to Turner, the work there alerted him to a condition of informational complexity in which 'the amount of information that can be generated or attended to with available resources is considerably less than the amount of information needed to describe fully or take account of the complexity of the situation' (Turner, 1976: 383). Although the extent to which the ideas just described were developed as provisional categories during the batch production study is not clear, these statements do suggest the 'following of ideas' that is characteristic of theoretical sampling. That Turner pursued these ideas in a second major study underscores the difficulties and the unlikeliness of researchers' exhausting all the theoretical possibilities raised in any one study.

In addition, these studies demonstrate what can be achieved when researchers diligently work to fragment and reduce their data through conceptualization. As I have related elsewhere (Locke, 1997), Turner's disaster studies (1978) demonstrate the naming and comparing activities that supported development of his theoretical categories. They underscore the power of creating something, for example, bringing into existence the idea and the fact of 'decoy phenomena,' through these activities.

Later adoption

The full adoption of the logic and practices of grounded theory continues to be evident into the 1980s and even into the 1990s. For example, in the early 1980s Burgelman (1983) adopted the grounded theory approach to study internal corporate venturing. To understand this activity, Burgelman collected data over a 15 month period of time on six ongoing internal corporate venturing projects that were in various stages of development in the new venture division of one high technology firm. His data documents comprised various slices of information. These included archival data from the division's charters and job descriptions and notes taken on the corporate long range plans for the division and each of the six projects. A total of 61 interviews were conducted with participants in the various internal corporate venturing projects, including division administrators as well as individuals in the firm's operating divisions and corporate management. Finally, some informal observations were made during time spent at the research site. Burgelman's description of his analytic process draws attention to a number of features of the grounded theory approach. He specifically mentions ignoring any existing theorizing about the process, the comparative analysis of the six projects, and the ongoing use of memoing where interpretations and insights about collected data were recorded in 'idea booklets' (Burgelman, 1983: 225). The outcome of the research was a stage model of the internal corporate venturing process that detailed the activities of project leaders, the venture division managers and corporate executives across four venture development phases.

Adaptation of the grounded theory approach

While published studies indicate that qualitative researchers have adopted and continue to adopt the grounded theory style of research to organize their analytic approach, its adaptation through selection and combination is a more prevalent phenomenon. In adaptation, researchers selectively integrate the logic and practices of other qualitative research styles with those of grounded theory. It is tempting to assume that adaptation of the grounded theory approach in management and organizational studies took place over time. But, variations in interpretation and adaptations of the approach were evident even in the 1970s. Let us look at two of them.

Early adaptation
In a study that was published as an award-winning paper, Dunn and Swierczek (1977) combined what they called a retrospective case analysis with the procedures of content analysis and grounded theory building to examine understanding of successful planned change efforts. From their research account, it appears that Dunn and Swierczek followed the purposeful tenets of initial theoretical sampling in selecting for study 67 cases describing a broad range of organizational change efforts. Having selected their sample, they developed a set of categories through two processes. Using existing theory as their guide, they created a set of variables with which to content analyze the cases. This content analysis was complemented by a theory building one in which they also inductively examined the cases and reformulated concepts. These concepts and variables were assembled into a coding instrument that outside coders, who had been trained on the instrument, used to analyze the 67 cases. Statistical analyses were applied to the results of the second phase of content analyses as a test of existing hypotheses about factors associated with successful planned change.

In this early study, the authors identify their work as consistent with the general purposes of grounded theory in that it took the examination of empirical data, albeit from secondary sources, as a central step in developing theoretical generalizations about successful planned change. Additionally, they argue that such generalizations will be more closely tied to their practical contexts. They relied on published case studies as a source of data, an approach that Strauss and Corbin (1990) acknowledge provides the researcher with a secondary source of materials from interviews and field notes as well as descriptive material on events and actions. The study made use of grounded theory's research procedures in two ways. First, they relied on the tenets of theoretical or purposeful sampling in their initial selection of cases. Specifically, cases were selected based on variation in terms of type of organization, societal type, and success in the reported outcome of the change effort. Second, some concept development is evident in their effort to reformulate concepts in light of their analysis of the cases.

At about the same time, Reis Louis (1977) drew on the grounded theory approach to develop a model of what happens as individuals conceptualize a conflict episode. As did Dunn and Swierczek, Reis Louis identifies with grounded theory on the basis that her aims are directed towards theory generation. Representing her approach as a 'modified version,' she developed her conflict conceptualization categories from an examination of an array of available theoretical literature on conflict. The ongoing information seeking characteristic of theoretical sampling is evident in her decision to search relevant literatures for information on personal factors and on potential steps in the process. In a sense her modification draws on the analytic procedures of grounded theory to conduct a form of meta-analysis of available literature.

Later adaptation
While the particular modification of the grounded theory approach presented by Reis Louis does not appear to be prevalent to this day, the practice of selecting and combining various analytic procedures evident in the Dunn and Swierczek study continues. One theme of adaptation seems to be the choice to bring more ordering and structuring mechanisms into the analytic process to reduce the ambiguity associated with confronting hundreds of pages of unstructured data. Another, more recent theme has been combination of grounded theory procedures with broader theoretical perspectives or schools of thought borrowed from other social science disciplines and even the humanities.

Selection and combination in research procedures Cautioned by warnings against the real possibility of being overwhelmed by the sheer volume of unstructured data (e.g. Miles, 1979), a number of organization and management scholars begin their analysis with some prior specification of existing theory to narrow and direct their analysis. The theory is, however, subject to change based on the data gathered. For example, Harris and Sutton (1986) describe meetings in which they worked to develop a rough working framework prior to and during the initial weeks of data gathering on the functions of parting ceremonies. Similarly, Eisenhardt and Bourgeois (1988) took a number of constructs from the literature on decision making into their research sites, measuring them in interview protocols and questionnaires.

Prior theory is also specified in Yin's (1984, 1994) strategy for the design of case studies. Sampling proceeds on the theoretical grounds of prior substantive theory. A case is chosen because it offers the opportunity of (a) testing prior theory by replicating previous cases, (b) extending theory by choosing cases that provide the opportunity of filling in theoretical formulations, or (c) extending theory by choosing cases that are the polar opposite of previous cases. A number of researchers have found appealing the replication logic which underlies this sampling strategy, and combine this sampling guide with grounded theory procedures for theorizing possible extensions. Such studies include Pandit's (1996) analysis of corporate turnaround, Eisenhardt's studies of decision making (Eisenhardt 1989a; Eisenhardt and Bourgeois, 1988), Inkpen and Dinur's (1998) investigation of knowledge management in international joint ventures and Poole's (1998) study of the discrepancy between words and deeds during organizational change.

It is important to underscore that when management and organization researchers choose to specify substantive theoretical constructs prior to their empirical work, they are deciding to let prior theory set the terms for what they will find – even if their research challenges that theory. Howard Becker (1986b) offers some insight into how existing theorizing can constrain our potential to achieve understanding from his own early research on drug use noted in Chapter 2. Becker tells the story of this research experience as a case in which, even though he set out to challenge existing theory about marijuana use, the latter nevertheless set the terms for his thinking. Specifically, Becker was interested in challenging the prevailing idea that people who used marijuana were engaging in 'weird' behavior which could be explained when researchers were able to identify those discrete psychological traits or sociological attributes that separated the 'weird' users from 'normal' non-users. He wanted to show that 'normal' people would engage in such behavior if the circumstances were right. According to Becker, in his eagerness to show that the literature was wrong, he could not perceive what his research was really about, namely, how people learn to define their own internal experiences. He speaks of this constraint, potentially imposed by preceding work in an area, as allowing the literature to 'deform your argument' (1986b: 149). Accordingly, the likelihood of inventing a new way to understand a phenomenon is reduced.

I should note, however, that although the emphasis in the 1967 monograph was on discovering *new* theory that was empirically grounded, Strauss (1970) indicated quite early on that its analytic style could also be used in the context of previously developed theory – as long as it had been carefully grounded in research. He argued that grounded theory could be used to extend previous theory and make it more dense by filling in what had been left out – that is by extending and refining its existing theoretical categories and relationships. In a demonstration of his keen ability to think in comparative terms, Strauss illustrated his point by decomposing a substantive theory about strained interaction with the visibly handicapped into its constituent elements and suggesting avenues of theoretical extension and possible sampling situations for each.

In addition to specifying theoretical constructs, a number of researchers have selected and combined some intermediate data reduction and ordering mechanisms with other grounded theory building procedures. For example, Eisenhardt advocates the use of what she terms 'within case analysis' (1989b: 540). This essentially involves the production of a descriptive write-up or 'case study' for each research site. These case studies are analogous to what Van Maanen (1979) called first-order accounts in that they describe the 'facts' or observable properties of the researched situation, including the interpretations organization members have of their own behavior. Having produced these case studies, researchers can focus their efforts at assigning meaning on these accounts rather than on the 'raw data.' For example, Gersick (1988) developed a case history for each of the task teams she studied, creating a document that contained what she described as detailed minutes of each meeting held by the teams over their life span. Leaving behind the raw data, her analysis then focused on these team cases histories. In them, the 'complete string of each team's meetings were closely examined in order to identify substantive themes of discussion and patterns of group behavior that persisted across meetings and to see when those themes and patterns ceased or changed' (Gersick, 1988: 15). The practice of constant comparison was used to identify similarities and differences in the meetings across all the team case histories.

Similarly, in their study of continuous change, Brown and Eisenhardt reduced the data they gathered from interviews, questionnaires, observations and archival sources in 9 strategic business units into 9 individual case studies. They described this process in the following terms: 'we entered all transcribed responses into a database indexed by case, interview number, interview type, and question number. Next we constructed a single version of both the high- and low-level interviews for each case by collecting all responses to the same question together as a single response. Using these interviews and secondary sources, we wrote a case study for each site' (1997: 5). (For each case, or SBU, they conducted an average of 9 interviews). Again, these case studies became the basis for theorizing.

As is the case with drawing on prior substantive theory, management and organization researchers should be aware of what we might be leaving behind when we amend grounded theory's analytic procedures. In the grounded theory approach, data reduction occurs through conceptualization. When researchers perform an intermediate data reduction on their data, they create data documents that are yet one more step removed from the empirical situations they studied. As I indicated in Chapter 5's discussion of theoretical sampling, analysts will often double back on their data documents and find theoretical implications in words and phrases that they had previous overlooked. The question arises, then, about what is potentially lost when researchers perform intermediate data reductions in advance of conceptualization. Certainly, the possibility is real of bypassing the kinds of nuanced micro processes of social behavior that are indicated in, say, the turn of a phrase that researchers notice after weeks of naming and comparing.

A number of researchers also draw on the data visualization mechanisms detailed by Miles and Huberman (1984) to assist their analytic process. For example, Sutton and Callahan (1987) created cross-site display tables that visualized various slices of data across the four organizations they studied for various categories. For example, a cross-site display was created for the category of audience response to filing 'chapter 11 bankruptcy status.' The table listed the various responses, for example, disengagement, indicated their presence across the four organizations, and provided illustrating data. Zbaracki (1998) similarly relied on data visualizing displays to support his analysis of TQM.

Selection and combination in theoretical schools of thought   Chapter 1 ended with a remark about the plurality evident in qualitative research and the crossing of boundaries between the humanities and the social sciences. An interesting development in grounded theory building has been the adoption of different schools of thought from which researchers might take a perspective on their research subject. Recall Glaser and Strauss's commitment to symbolic interactionism.

In our studies of writing practices (Golden-Biddle and Locke, 1993; Locke and Golden-Biddle, 1997), as mentioned before, we have relied on the perspective offered by social constructionism and rhetorical theory to help us pay attention to writing. Whereas we were naturally accustomed to examining words on a page for what they were saying, informed by these points of view on the social world, we understood and were able to examine words for what they were doing. These schools of thought provided us with an orientation to our data without specifying what we would perceive in it. For the latter, we relied on grounded theory's procedures.

In a similar combination of a broad theoretical perspective with grounded theory's analytic procedures, Coopey, Keegan and Emler (1998) use structuration theory as an orienting framework to understand innovation because its point of view on social actions links organizational and individual levels of analysis. They indicate that structuration theory draws attention to the patterning of social relations; it attends to the rules and resources and the norms and procedures that regulate resource use on the part of organizational members. Furthermore, this perspective also underscores that these practices, in turn, reinforce and reproduce the very organization structures that form the context for innovation. In terms of data, they derived their sampling logic from Patton's (1987) idea of maximizing variety, and interviewed 30 managers who had introduced innovations and who represented a wide range of hierachical levels, functions and experience in three firms. This logic is, of course, also consistent with the idea that theoretical sampling across diverse contexts is likely to result in higher levels of generality in researchers' conceptualizing. Their primary data set comprised these interviews and they were supplemented with interviews of another 44 individuals who had collaborated in the innovations. Grounded theory's procedures for generating categories and theoretical sampling within a data set were used to assign meaning to the interview narratives. The researchers began by intensively analyzing 15 of the innovator interview narratives with a view towards creating conceptual categories. Then 14 categories that were indicated by the highest proportion of individual innovation stories formed the basis for theoretical sampling within the remaining data set.

A small group of studies demonstrate adaptation along the lines of both procedure and school of thought bringing a definite eclecticism to grounded theorizing. In his study of the Canadian gas pipeline explosion, Gephart (1993) employs ethnomethodology as an informing school of thought. It draws attention to the practices though which people involved in situations create the sense that they share a common framework of meaning for understanding the world. This theoretical perspective oriented him to the sense-making activities of relevant actors as they are expressed in their discourse, and also directed his attention to key sense-making resources on which individuals draw. Thus, Gephart directed his attention to understanding those resources, posing such questions as, '[W]hat are the important concepts and terms, or vocabularies, used by organization members in inquiry-based sense-making about disasters?' (1993: 1475). His data gathering logic and procedures were informed by ethnography's practice of ongoing involvement and participation, as he attended the public inquiry in its entirety, and by grounded theory's logic of sampling for theoretical purposes. Following the latter, he chose for analytic attention the testimony and remarks of three constituents, gas company management, pipeline workers and government, because they were the major theoretically meaningful groups involved in the inquiry. To create and assign meaning to his data set, though, Gephart (1993) relied on other procedures. He used a word-processor based procedure to locate the incidence of key words and to create data exhibits of them in context, thereby reducing the various slices of data he had gathered over the course of the inquiry. Further, Cicourel's expansion analysis (cited in Gephart, 1993) supported and informed his analytic efforts to assign meaning to those data exhibits.

In a final example, the study of mentoring and management by objectives in the big six public accounting firms by Covaleski et al. (1998) is similarly eclectic in its theoretical orientation and procedures. These authors adopt a more critical perspective on management and organizations by relying on Foucault's ideas about power, knowledge, and the constitution of the self. These direct their research and analytic attention. They invoke five Foucauldian methodological injunctions that give shape to their study. One injunction with its resultant impact on the study follows. '[R]ather than focus on who exercises power and why, attention should be placed on how it is exercised, power in a direct and immediate relationship with its target; we focused on the application of disciplinary and avowal techniques to firm line partners' (Covaleski et al., 1998: 304). They selected management by objectives and mentoring as forms of disciplinary and avowal techniques, respectively. With Foucault's ideas helping to direct what they should attend to, Covaleski et al. (1998) engaged in a prolonged data gathering effort consistent with ethnographic principles of involvement. They describe grounded theory logic as informing their investigative efforts because it underscores the reciprocal relationship between their data gathering and theory development efforts.

The same plurality that is evident in qualitative research in general is clearly evident in the adoption and adaptation of the grounded theory research style in management and organization studies.

The kinds of grounded theory researchers have developed

The same plurality increasingly evident in the schools of thought and procedures that comprise grounded theory building is evident in the kinds of theory that management and organization researchers are developing. This variation in the form and shape of their theories is consistent with Glaser's (1978) ideas that researchers would flexibly draw on and construct frameworks based on the theoretical leads suggested by their data, rather than pursuing the achievement of a particular theoretical framework. As such, the theories also underscore Weick's (1995) notions of theoretical elements as 'in process theorizing' that nevertheless serve as place markers in understanding about a phenomenon.

From the theoretical outputs of researchers who have pursued the grounded theory style of research there is little evidence of a predominant comprehensive theoretical scheme suggested, for example, by Strauss's (1987) coding paradigm or Glaser's '6 C's' framework. Rather the theoretical products are more limited and more varied. That said, whether the research was pursued by adopting or adapting the approach, grounded theorizing in management and organization studies does seem to result in action oriented theoretical products. Chapter 3 discussed the increasing interest management researchers are showing in composing process or action oriented theories, but it seems that those pursuing grounded theorizing have focused on process all along. Their theoretical products capture movement in organizational life by theorizing select action relationships and also movement through time. When viewed from the perspective of coding paradigms, these are usually more limited renditions of the kinds of theoretical category and relationship suggested by the more comprehensive paradigms. Some examples are in order.

Of the studies that I reviewed, Orlikowski's (1993) theoretical framework most closely approximates that suggested by a comprehensive coding paradigm. It accounts for the adoption of CASE tools through a slightly limited rendition of Strauss's (1987) and Strauss and Corbin's (1990) coding paradigm. There is a clear focus on action in terms of both the managerial actions that create the conditions for introducing CASE

tools to an organization and the action strategies that comprise implementation. However, it also maps the institutional context for adoption
which itself comprises three contexts, namely, the organization's environment, the organization itself, and its information systems situation. And,
it describes the impact or consequences of adopting CASE tools on the
firms' clients' managers, and system developers. By delineating contextual features, conditions, action strategies and consequences surrounding adoption, the theoretical framework explains adoption in
terms of the context in which it occurs, the conditions that cause or
initiate it, the actions that execute it and the consequences that follow. As
an aside, it is worth noting that to 'complete' Strauss's coding paradigm,
Orlikowski would also have had to pursue further theoretical sampling
and analysis to identify the intervening conditions that would alter
managers' decisions to pursue CASE tools. She would have had to
determine how the consequences that followed adoption subsequently
influenced managers' ongoing commitments to CASE tools or other
similar systems and how those consequences affected the strategies they
would use to introduce such technologies into the organization. Needless
to say, that would be a rather daunting task, and its completion within
the scope of a single study would be highly unlikely.

From the above description, the Orlikowski study obviously paid
attention to and conceptualized a number of contextual features as they
impact action. By contrast, Eisenhardt's (1989a) study of how senior
management makes fast strategic decisions frames this process in terms
of a causes/consequences model, narrowing her focus instead on the
behaviors through which speed is achieved and the consequences that
result from it. She identifies five categories of senior executive behavior
as causal agents. These are: their use of real time information; simultane-
ous consideration of multiple decision alternatives; reliance on experienced counselors; pursuit of decision integration; and use of a qualified
consensus seeking style with their senior management team. These
behaviors variously result in three mediating conditions that lead to
increased decision speed: accelerated cognitive processing and increased
confidence to act on the part of senior executives, and smoother group
process within the executive team. Further, the model causally relates
decision-making speed to firm performance. Each of these relationships
is expressed in propositional form.

The study of how management and organization researchers create
opportunity for contribution in the journal articles reporting their findings (Locke and Golden-Biddle, 1997) essentially composes an 'action
strategies' scheme – albeit within a social constructionist framework
where the action strategies take place on paper. Our theoretical framework conceptualizes four layers of textual action. The first, most general,
level is made up of two core actions or processes. A second level
articulates three variations in each of those core processes. A third level

conceptualizes the textual acts through which each variation is constituted. And (finally!), a fourth level details the language practices that
characterized those acts. For example, one of the variations of the core
process of creating an organized depiction of the literature was progressive coherence – the portrayal of our understanding of a certain
phenomenon as advancing steadily. One of the textual acts that
shows progressive coherence is the construction of consensus among
researchers, and this is textually constituted through use of phrases such
as 'there is considerable agreement.'

A further expression of the interest in creating theoretical schemes that
capture action is evident in the increasing visibility of stage of phase
models as outcomes of grounded theory building efforts. Among early
grounded theory studies, although Turner's (1976) theoretical contribution essentially offers a conditions/consequences framework, it is located
in the 'incubation' and 'precipitating event' phases of a six-stage model
of disaster development.

Stage models are the analytic and theoretical outcome in many other
grounded theory studies, and they are developed at all levels of organizational analysis. Within these models, organizational researchers are
investing effort in putting the stages in motion, so to speak, by identifying the mechanisms that trigger or facilitate movement from one stage to
the next. For example, focused on the organizational level of analysis,
Burgelman's (1983) model of how internal corporate venturing occurs
describes the actions that constitute each of four phases of this activity
(defining new business opportunities, impetus, integration into corporate strategy, and structuring an internal selection environment). He also
identifies actions taken by key stakeholders that shift venturing activity
from one stage to the next. For example, product championing activity on the part of venture project managers moves the process from the
opportunity definition to the impetus phase; organizational championing
by the new venture division's management facilitates movement to the
phase where the project becomes integrated into corporate strategy; and
selecting activity on the part of the new venture division's and corporate
management moves venturing from the phase of integration into corporate strategy to structuring.

At the individual level, Kram's (1983) study of mentoring proposes
that a mentoring relationship passes through four phases (initiation,
cultivation, separation and redefinition), and it identifies various psychological and organizational factors that cause movement into a new phase.
For example, her theory suggests that a growing desire to work auton-
omously on the part of a junior manager is one of the triggers for moving
away from the cultivation phase and into separation.

And, at the group level, Gersick's (1988) study of the development of
task groups, previously mentioned, conceives of group development as
progressing through three discernible phases: an initial inertial phase
which comprises approximately half of a group's calendar time and

which takes its shape from the first group meeting; a discrete mid-point transition; and a third phase, again of inertial movement. The model suggests that the trigger for movement is a temporal one: the group recognizes that it is approaching the midpoint between the time it began and its task deadline. Movement into the final phase of task completion is engendered by plans created for the completion of work during the transitional phase.

Several other instances of theoretical outcomes being framed as stage models are found: Zbaracki's (1998) study of the adoption of TQM; Hargadon and Sutton's (1997) study of how product development innovation occurs through technology brokering across industries; Gioia and Chittipeddi's (1991) analysis of a large university's strategic change effort; Isabella's (1990) investigation of how managers make sense of organizational events as change unfolds; and Fox-Wolfgramm, Boal and Hunt's (1998) study of prospector and defender bank adaptation to institutional change.

While static theoretical models are generally in the minority, they do occupy a space in grounded theorizing in management and organization studies. For example, Lee, MacDermid and Buck (2000) drew on grounded theory's analytic techniques to investigate the implications of reduced load work arrangements for professionals and managers, and their theoretical scheme distinguishes three types of organizational response. Through their analysis of interview data, they generated three distinct paradigms that account for different ways that organizations understand and implement these work arrangements. These paradigms are constituted through a number of key dimensions that describe differences in the stance that employers took towards reduced load work arrangements, including their rationale for supporting it, and in the employer's understanding of the responsibility for negotiating and managing such arrangements.

Lyles and Mitroff's (1980) study of problem formulation is also an instance of such a theoretical product. These researchers conceptualized problem formulation in terms of three typologies: the types of problem manager's faced, the method of inquiry their organizations used in formulating problems, and themes that characterize the problem formulation process.

I should like to bring to a close this discussion of the forms that theoretical products take by noting that some researchers form their theorized elements quite differently. For example, Brown (1998) sets aside the kinds of theoretical configuration that invite schematization and composes three 'narratives' which account for competing groups' efforts to maintain legitimacy in the face of a failing information system's implementation project. I would hope that grounded theory researchers would not approach their analytic task with the presumption that they had to generate theoretical elements that could be expressed in boxes and arrows. Such outcomes would likely not fit, for example, with feminist or critical adaptations of grounded theory. I think it is inappropriate to put that constraint on the form that potential theorizing might take. There is room in grounded theory building for researchers to compose their theoretical products in a variety of ways constrained only by their creativity and the plausible interpretation of their data.

Constraints on the grounded theory approach

The grounded theory approach originated in studies of formal work organizations and is appealing on several grounds to managerial and organizational scholars, but the questions arises as to whether research in formal organizations and on the people who manage them engenders problems that are in any sense unique. While this is doubtful, several researchers have suggested that there are a number of major issues that are brought into sharper relief when the research site is the corporate setting and the research subjects occupy positions of power (Laurila, 1997; Thomas, 1993). For example, Bulmer (1988) suggests that establishing a workable data-gathering role and moving across units in the organization can be a challenge. Easterby-Smith, Thorpe and Lowe (1991) underscore the politics and ethical issues associated with conducting research in formal organizations and on managers in particular. The most salient area of concern with regards to executing the grounded theory approach centers on the issue of access, especially as it relates to the open-ended pursuit of theoretical sampling. This is likely to be highest when researchers are pursuing their data gathering via participant-observation as compared with other less invasive data gathering practices.

While access to medical institutions was unproblematic to Glaser and Strauss, who appeared to have unrestrained and long term access to their research sites, for most organization scholars, this is can be a problematic issue. Gaining access to the reserach site as well as to the particular groups and individuals that it may be most relevant to study are recurrent concerns. For those researchers who require the type of access necessary to conduct participant observation and who wish to do so at multiple organizations, the problems may be most acute. Barley (1990) describes the time and the lengths he went through to gain and negotiate access to the two hospital sites for his participant-observation based data gathering – a process that took five months of persistent effort to accomplish.

Once in the organization, the issues of access persists when researchers pursue theoretical sampling in the flexible open-ended form articulated in the original monograph. The level of access in which researchers want to gain entry in a way that grants them entry to all groups, departments or individuals that may be relevant, is likely hard to come by. At the same time, once in, they are in a better position to negotiate further access. For example, once I had gained intial access to the hospital that was the site for my dissertation, and settled into a routine of participant observation, gaining access to other departments and groups was accomplished fairly easily.

While there may be issues associated with gaining access, grounded theory's central practice of overlapping data collection and analysis poses other problems. The practice of moving back and forth between data gathering and analysis means that researchers will be offsite for periods of time during data gathering. At the very least, the overlap of analysis and data collection means that researchers should give some explicit thought to how they might pace data collection. For example, they may decide to conduct one or two days of observation or two interviews a week. That expectation should, of course, be part of the entry negotiations.

Problems also arise from the need to maintain some continuity with the research setting. Indeed, in the original monograph, Glaser and Strauss suggest that researchers should not think twice about taking months off from data gathering if they need that time to think through their working theory, to clarify what additional data they need from ongoing data gathering efforts. This can result in difficulties associated with sustaining access once it has been granted. Interestingly, during an approximately seven-week offsite analytic period, Barley (1990) notes that he nevertheless returned to the site for one day every two weeks purely for the purposes of maintaining connections with personnel, of providing assurances that he would return, and to keep abreast of any major developments. This suggests a useful strategy for maintaining access to researchers taking time off from data gathering to pursue their analysis.

Issues associated with gaining the type of access necessary to commence and maintain theoretical sampling are real, the studies and approaches I examined over the course of writing this book suggest a number of interesting avenues that management and organization researchers might consider. For example, many of the studies already discussed sought and relied on archival sources of data that provided rich and detailed accounts of organizational and individual action. Theoretically, such data provide unlimited access from which to execute theoretical sampling. Turner's (1978) disaster study previously discussed provides an example of the use of publicly available inquiry reports as data bases. Gephart's (1993) study of a natural gas pipeline explosion in Canada similarly relies on public inquiry reports – the transcripts of official testimony made by court reporters, the government energy board's final report, and company documents to complement his informal interviewing carried out during the course of the inquiry from which to constitute his data documents. The perspectives of a number of key organization actors, for example, managers, pipeline crew members, and representatives from outside regulatory agencies, were captured and available in these data documents.

Yet another example is Orton's (1997) use of the resources of the Ford library to study the United States' Central Intelligence Agency. The library afforded a huge data base which included such potential data documents as minutes from meetings, decision documents, research summaries and press conferences. Clearly, such a range of possible data documents will allow for theoretical sampling to occur within the data base as well as provide opportunities for a variety of slices or sources of data. Additionally, the advent of the world wide web has increased and speeded up access to a variety of potential data bases. Not surprisingly, researchers are increasingly looking to the internet as a resource to access data. Pandit (1996), for example, describes the theoretical sampling strategy he followed to study corporate turnaround, using the internet to put together his data documents and to permit theoretical sampling across two empirical cases of organizational turnarounds. He relied on the internet, specifically Reuter's 'Textline' and Predicasts' 'PROMT', to compile a set of data documents made up of newspaper reports, trade and business journal articles, government publications, broker reviews, and annual company documents and press releases for each of his companies. With access under his control, so to speak, he began his analysis with Fisons PLC and then further developed his theorizing through data gathered on a second case, British Steel Corporation.

One other avenue of exploration involves taking the comparative dimension of theoretical sampling to an extreme degree, so that researchers are not always looking to study their phenomenon in large corporate settings with their associated barriers to entry and openness. Diane Vaughan's work is interesting in this regard. Vaughan (1992) reinterpreted and reapplied grounded theory's comparative logic to develop an approach to expanding on and elaborating previously developed theory. In this approach, which she refers to as 'theoretical elaboration,' she takes seriously the notion that general theories of a phenomenon can be developed in its empirical observation in a variety of organizational forms. Following Strauss's understanding of developing existing theory (1970), her approach begins by taking any theoretical element, be it a model or a particular concept, and using it to guide theoretical sampling of noticeably different comparative cases. Theoretical sampling, then, pursues significant variation in such criteria as size, complexity and function. Thus, in her work elaborating Merton's social structure and anomie theory into a broad theory of organizational misconduct, she examined very different expressions of misconduct. These included the Space Shuttle Challenger accident, police misconduct, and family violence. Vaughan underscores that the differences among the cases in levels and units of analysis (e.g. violence in the family versus a major accident at NASA) usually produce startling contrasts that challenge the analysts to dramatically reassess received theory.

Obviously I am not suggesting that access to the kinds of site Vaughan studied is unproblematic. However, her logic for selecting comparative sites raises possibilities for examining managerial phenomena in quite diverse settings. Certainly hierarchical for profit business organizations may be one site, with their attendant problems of access, but other sites which contrast in their complexity and size and in which similar processes might be explored might be more easily accessed. Her strategy certainly offers some interesting food for thought.

7

Writing grounded theory

Writing in the middle 1960s, Glaser and Strauss (1967) anticipated by almost 20 years some of the concerns with writing that drew scholar attention during qualitative research's fourth historical moment characterized as the crisis of representation. Their appreciation for the problematic dimensions of writing is reflected in understanding of the active role played by the reader in making meaning from research texts. Specifically, they noted that the reader makes the determination of whether researchers have developed a credible theoretical scheme. The reader scrutinizes the text to make an assessment of whether researchers' reported analytic work is adequate and likely factors in his or her own experiences to determine the validity and plausibility of the proposed theoretical scheme. In terms of writing practice, Glaser and Strauss (1967) pointed to the importance of writing manuscripts that richly illustrate the theory. For example, they underscored the importance of crafting written accounts that enable the reader to see and hear the actors in the studied social scene, but to do so in terms of the composed theoretical framework.

In this chapter, then, I focus on issues associated with writing grounded theoretical accounts for publication. My perspective on the writing process is explicitly rhetorical. That is, it follows the lead of such literary critics as Booth (1961) and Iser (1978, 1989), who argue that 'the hand of the writer and the eyes of the reader shape all written works, even those in science' (Golden-Biddle and Locke, 1997: 8). From this point of view, the manuscripts that we write in management and organization studies, as in any other discipline, are understood to be proposals for the grounded theoretical points composed through our research that we direct towards our disciplinary audience. Furthermore, a rhetorical stance also recognizes that, as authors, 'we write from an interested perspective; we have a personal stake in the outcomes of our work' (Golden-Biddle and Locke, 1997: 14). So, while we certainly write to explicate our developed theoretical framework, we also write to persuade our audience of its plausibility and its relevance to our understanding of management and organizations (Golden-Biddle and Locke, 1997).

The publication that I am concerned with is the journal article, because of its prominent role in the public discourse of researchers (Winsor, 1993;

Yearley, 1981) and in advancing and maintaining our careers as scholars of organizations and management (Golden-Biddle and Locke, 1997). We write our journal manuscripts so that our proposals of grounded theory will be taken as authoritative (Golden-Biddle and Locke, 1997; Spector and Kitsuse, 1977). This chapter will examine how, through our writing practices, we construct that authority. I am particularly interested in the authority derived from three sources through our writing. These are: demonstrating the 'groundedness' of our theoretical elements; being able to argue for the contribution our theoretical elements make to the wider theoretical issues in which our field has an interest; and showing 'good practice' in our accounts of the analytic operations performed.

Writing the groundedness of theoretical elements

Glaser and Strauss's recognition that researchers need to write the developed framework in such a manner as to allow readers to imaginatively see and hear the actors in the social scene in terms of the theoretical framework foreshadows two dimensions that Karen Golden-Biddle and I subsequently framed through our study of writing practices in management and organization studies. They are: achieving authenticity and a solid data theory coupling (Golden-Biddle and Locke, 1993, 1997), respectively.

To develop authenticity, readers need to be convinced that the authors were present to the world they studied and that they understood it from the actors' point of view. However, to achieve the solid data theory coupling that allows a theoretical element to be viewed as 'grounded,' that world has to be linked to researchers' theoretical framework. The challenge to authors, then, is to write data linked theoretical points.

Typically, this is accomplished through a style of presentation that moves back and forth between extensive theoretical presentations and illustrative 'live' excerpts from the setting. It alternates between 'telling' and 'showing,' as the manuscript attempts to take the reader analytically forward to the developed theoretical elements and back to the data fragments that instanced the theory (Booth, 1961; Golden-Biddle and Locke, 1997). Booth (1961) distinguished between showing and telling in the following manner that underscores the relationship between data and theory. For Booth, we 'show' in our writing when we present accurately observed detail, whether through our own authorial voice acting as narrator or when we speak though the voices of those actors in the research setting whose comments we have recorded. We 'tell' when we explain the significance of that detail. (While Booth was directing his comments towards the writing of literary texts, their relevance to the genre of scientific writing is obvious.)

Weaving together showing and telling to write data indicated theory
At the level of the 'results' section of the manuscript in which researchers present their theoretical schemes, the writing that constitutes a grounded presentation of theory weaves together data incidents and theoretical elements. The data incidents demonstrate that researchers authentically were present to and captured the realities of those they studied, while the theoretical points underscore that researchers understood the general significance of those particular incidents.

In Glaser and Strauss's original writings, they presented their findings in the form of an ongoing richly descriptive theoretical narrative, organized by the main categories of the framework. For example, in their article on dying as a non-scheduled status passage, they 'tell,' quite formally, the three stages of this passage and especially the work involved in each of those stages. Yet, their presentations involve such vivid detail that readers can easily place themselves imaginatively into the social scene. Below is an excerpt that describes the dimensions associated with the second stage, 'announcing the passage.'

> Since the behavior of others toward a status occupant is temporally oriented . . . it is crucially significant that announcement of dying, since it is an unscheduled status passage, be the obligation of the doctor . . . For in the end the doctor is the person held socially and perhaps legally responsible for the diverse outcomes resulting from changes in the behavior of the patient, of other parties to the patient's passage, and of the hospital organization occasioned by his legitimating and announcing temporal aspects of the dying. These outcomes can range from being most *beneficial*, as when the doctor announces to the staff that the patient is about to die in order to co-ordinate heroic measures to save him, to being most *adverse*, as when a family, unaware that their relative is dying, is thereby given no time to prepare for his death and may be deeply shocked by the surprise of it.
>   . . . In some hospitals, the doctor is required at least to legitimate for the medical staff a degree of the certainty dimension of the dying or transitional status by putting the patient on a critically, dangerously, or seriously ill list or by including the information on an admitting card. He will often be reminded of this rule 'before it is too late.' The patient's being posted on such a critical list usually requires an announcement of dying by the doctor to the family. If they are not on hand, a family member is sent a wire stating that 'your (kin) has been put on the critically ill list, please come at once'. (Glaser and Strauss, 1965a: 51, emphasis in original)

This extended excerpt shows clearly the interweaving of formal theoretical elements with an almost painfully detailed showing of the social scene. Theoretical elements are evident in the impingement of structure on the control of the announcement, in the range of outcomes that follow on from an announcement, the actions through which announcements are made, and so on. But, these elements are all instanced by specific details of the social scene, as in the case of the possible adverse outcome associated with the announcement. Often, these details of the social scene are shown in the narrator's voice; at other times, they are shown through the voices of the scene's actors, as in the case of the doctor being reminded to follow the rules 'before it is too late.'

In management and organization studies, the presentation of grounded theories similarly follows a format that involves the telling of theoretical elements and the showing of data fragments that instance them. Let us look at an example. Isabella's (1990) presentation of the grounded theory she developed about how managers make sense of organizational events as change unfolds follows a format that echoes Glaser and Strauss's approach and that has become common in such theory building studies. This format can be outlined as: summarize the theoretical frame – serially present each theoretical element well illus-trated with data instances – summarize the theoretical frame. Typical of stage oriented process theories, her theoretical scheme delineates a number of distinct stages that characterize how managers make sense over time. And, it identifies the processes or triggers that move indi-viduals from one stage to another. She begins her presentation with a focus on her theory, summarizing the stages of managerial sense-making and the elements that constitute each stage in the following way.

> The data from this research revealed that interpretations of key events evolve through a series of stages – anticipation, confirmation, culmination, and aftermath. A different construed reality, set of interpretive tasks and pre-dominant frame of reference characterize each stage. During anticipation, managers assemble rumors and other tidbits of information into an in-progress frame of reference. During confirmation . . . (Isabella, 1990: 14).

Having presented her readers with this summary, she then moves on to detail each stage, drawing in the comments made by the managers she interviewed. Headings are used to underscore each element. For exam-ple, under the heading, 'Anticipation,' she writes:

> Countless rumors, hunches, suspicions, and scattered bits of information pulled together as well as possible characterize the collective interpretations representing the first interpretational stage . . .
>
> The construed reality at this stage is composed of both rumors and discon-nected pieces of information . . . In general, these rumors were neither malicious nor fantastic; they were 'bogies' expressing fear or anxiety about what might or might not occur (Rosnow and Fine, 1976: 23). There were rumors about the names of possible acquirers, possible sites for a new corporate headquarters, and possible structural changes designed to deal with declining service:
>
> *A common rumor of takeover was American Express* (acquisition).
>
> *For a while, I was hearing rumors that the company would relocate out to the suburbs* (relocation).
>
> *Our services were down; there were lots of complaints. Everyone suspected something was going to happen* (commitment to quality). (Isabella, 1990: 16)

Her writing here weaves together telling the theory and showing her data in a number of ways. The theoretical stage is told in the heading, in her statements regarding its constituent elements (in this case rumor), and in the variations of the category rumor. She imaginatively takes the reader to the social reality she encountered by showing both through her own voice and the voices of organization members the variety of rumors swirling around the organization that she encountered in their interview accounts. Thus, examples of the data incidents that she drew on to develop her theoretical elements are woven into her presentation of them. This way of writing the theory strongly invites the reader to see the closeness of the relationship between data and theory – to perceive its groundedness. Isabella shows additional data in tables that are organized by the theoretical elements, again underscoring the link between theory and empirical reality.

Following the detailed presentation of each theoretical element, Isabella again presents the complete theoretical framework, including a visualization of it through the use of a figure, underscoring the theory that she has developed. This basic format of summary of theory – serial illustrated presentation of theory – summary of theory – is evident across a number of grounded theory building studies. Visual depictions of the theory through figures are common, though it appears to be a matter of researcher choice as to whether they are presented initially or at the conclusion of the grounded theory presentation. Other articles following this form include Sutton and Callahan (1987), Eisenhardt (1989a), Kahn (1993), Locke and Golden-Biddle (1997) and Coopey, Keegan and Emler (1998).

This format is, as I indicated, fairly standard in presentations of grounded theory in studies of organization and management, though there are some variations. The writing practice of setting apart from their narrative those data fragments that are shown through the voices of organizational members, whether in their conversations or as they are inscribed in organizational documents, allows researchers to write into their accounts more of the data. This is particularly the case when they also show data in tables. Tables also allow researchers to underscore the groundedness of their data, by showing, for example, fragments express-ing theoretical elements across various slices of data. In my study on comedy and the management of emotions, I was able to use tables to array data fragments from three sources, archival materials, participant observation and semi-structured interviews (Locke, 1996) to instance particular theoretical elements. Hargadon and Sutton (1997) similarly use tables to present slices of data from a broad array of sources.

Some authors, though, choose to narrate their theory and data, pre-dominantly in their own voice. Their accounts are told in the voice of an informed narrator/author. For example, the data that instanced Turner's theoretical framework is presented in his own voice, in paraphrase form. An instance that he provides of the category 'decoy phenomena' is 'local residents mistakenly thought that the danger from tips at Aberfan was associated with the tipping of very fine waste, and they withdrew some of their complaints when it was agreed that this would not be tipped' (1976: 392). In a variation of this, Burgelman (1983) presents his theory of internal corporate venturing largely through his own voice. He does show some 'raw' data fragments but, interestingly, they are presented in side notes in the margins of the article.

Finally, authors occasionally choose to present their theory in more formal terms, for example through the use of propositions. As an instance, following his presentation of his theory about the process of strategic business exit, Burgelman (1994) offers a number of summary formal theoretical propositions. Similarly, Eisenhardt and Bourgeois include the presentation of formal propositions as part of their serial narration of their theory of politics in strategic decision making in high velocity environments. An illustration is:

> Executives do not shift allies as issues change, particularly in politically active teams. Rather, they develop stable coalitions with one or possibly two other executives. They routinely seek out alliances with the same people. When usual allies disagree on an issue, they generally do not seek out more favorably disposed executives. Rather they either drop the issue or pursue their interests alone.
>   *Proposition 3: The greater the use of politics within a top management team, the greater the likelihood of stable alliance patterns.* (1988: 753–754, emphasis in original)

The traditional format for the scientific article locates its 'findings' in the third 'results' section following a presentation of the literature and description of methods used. Obviously a research account that begins with a presentation of the literature mimics the hypothetico-deductive approach in which theory is *a priori*. In an interesting move, increasingly organization researchers who engage in theory building work are subverting this format by introducing raw data into the beginning of the manuscript. Following the customary abstract, rather than move directly into a consideration of the literature, a number of authors are choosing to present some raw data carefully chosen to highlight key theoretical points that they will be making when they present their theory (Golden-Biddle and Locke, 1997). This showing of data in the opening page of the article not only foreshadows the theory to come but also it clearly invites the reader to view the study as one that begins with particularistic empirical observations; it is theory-building in character.

For example, Sutton and Callahan provide a sneak preview to their theorization of how bankruptcy spoils the image of top managers and firms by presenting this excerpt from an interview with a former CEO immediately following their abstract. 'My reputation was smirched. It was as if I had committed some sort of sin. I feel guilty. I will never be able to get [venture capital] funding again. I will never get another chance to be CEO' (1987: 405, brackets in original). Similarly, Pratt and

Rafaeli (1997) follow the abstract with the following excerpts from interviews with two different nurses in their study of how organization members used dress to present and negotiate various issues related to the identity of the nursing unit and the nursing profession,

> Patients who wear pajamas, and see hospital garb around them think of themselves as sick. If *they and their caretakers wear street clothes*, patients will think of themselves as moving out of the sick role, and into rehabilitation. They will be ready for life outside the hospital. This is the rehab philosophy, and this is what makes this unit unique.
> (Head nurse of a rehabilitation unit; emphasis ours.)

> We are medical and health professionals. We do professional work. We take care of sick patients, we deal with their bodily fluids, and get their slime all over us. So we should all look like medical professionals, *we should be dressed in scrubs*.
> (Nurse on the evening shift of the same unit; emphasis ours; Pratt and Rafaeli, 1997: 862–898.)

By italicizing key and contrasting phrases in each excerpt, the authors orient the readers to the contradictory meanings and competing identities expressed in dress that will be the focus of their theorizing.

Writing in the literature

In the hypothetico-deductive model of science, researchers begin their study of a phenomenon with the literature. Specifying ignorance about what is not yet known but needs to be learned in order to further advance knowledge is one of the cornerstones of good scientific practice in this model (Merton, 1987). Accordingly, the standard format for the journal article reflects this assumption, with the literature appearing as its first section (Knorr-Cetina, 1981). But, what happens to how we write the literature when we begin with empirical data and hold existing knowledge in abeyance until our theoretical frameworks are well developed? The answer seems to be that the literature that establishes the phenomenon to be investigated still appears at the beginning of the manuscript, even though it may be preempted by a sneak peek into the investigated scene as just discussed. Indeed, in Glaser and Strauss's dying studies, some literature does appear in their opening paragraphs as they introduce their audience to the phenomenon they studied. However, writing the literature in grounded theory differs from the traditional model in that literature is sometimes integrated into the presentation of the model in what is usually the 'findings' section of the manuscript. Furthermore, the relationship between their grounded theoretical frame and a broader literature to which it makes a contribution is sometimes a problematic issue, because the research questions are not usually framed in terms of existing theory.

When discussing the literature to which a study is written as making a contribution, Karen Golden-Biddle and I found it useful to draw on the metaphor of story and to use it to distinguish between what we termed field-based stories and theoretical stories (Golden-Biddle and Locke, 1997). The field-based story is the grounded theoretical framework developed through the authors' analytic interaction with their data – the grounded theory. In this way of thinking, a developed grounded theory is a field-based story. The theoretical story, on the other hand, is based in existing theoretical conversations in our field. It identifies that area of management and organization studies, for instance, institutional theory, organization learning, sense-making, service management or whatever, to which researchers' grounded theorizing can make a contribution.

Writing the literature back in to the field-based story
As indicated in Chapter 4's discussion of the logic of the grounded theory approach, researchers integrate existing literature on the substantive topic into their thinking as the theoretical categories and framework stabilize. During memoing at the later stages of category development, they write in that literature that has a bearing on the conceptual categories and their relations. Accordingly, when researchers write up their grounded theories or field-based stories for publication, a number of scholars choose to integrate relevant existing literature into their presentations of data indicated theoretical elements.

As an illustration, look at how Hargadon and Sutton (1997) write their grounded field-based story of how innovation occurs through technology brokering by integrating their theoretical presentation with data from the research site and relevant existing works from the literature. In this excerpt, they are presenting the first phase of technology brokering. During this 'access' phase, gaps in the flow of information between industries provide opportunities for individuals who are exposed to technology from one industry to imagine yet unforeseen applications for it in another.

> . . . The transfer of potentially valuable technologies to other industries, when it occurs, can cause significant economic and competitive changes (Schumpeter, 1934; Rosenberg, 1982), but gaps in the flow of information across industry boundaries often prevent this diffusion. Organizations like IDEO, by occupying positions within multiple industries, may bridge these gaps.
>   IDEO's access to outside industries offers an advantage to clients who want new product innovations. IDEO's designers have generated part of all of over 3,000 new product designs for clients since its formation in 1978 . . . IDEO does not maintain a database of clients by industry, but our research indicates it has worked in over 40 industries. From these industries, IDEO's designers have typically seen a broader range of technologies than clients with experience in only one of a few industries. The network concept of range describes the extent to which an actor contacts a diversity of other actors, and can be

measured in two ways, as volume of contacts or as quality of contacts (Burt, 1983). . . . The evidence summarized in Table 2 suggests that IDEO's value as a technology broker depends not only on the number of clients and industries it works with (volume of contacts), but also on the technologies in those industries that are potentially valuable yet previously unknown in others (quality of contacts). IDEO's methodology handbook recognizes this value: 'Working with companies in such dissimilar industries as medical instruments, furniture, toys, and computers has given us a broad view of the latest technologies, materials and components available' (Hargadon and Sutton, 1997: 728–729)

In this extended excerpt we see how theoretical notions about occupying a position within multiple industries may provide organizations opportunities to access a broad range of information presented with data that demonstrate the groundedness of this claim (for example, the fragment from the employee handbook). And, that same theoretical notion is integrated with existing ideas from economic theory and also from network theory. Indeed, in this particular manuscript, integration of theory and prior work into the presentation of the grounded process model of technology brokering is extensive. It therefore represents one extreme on a range of how extensively theory is integrated into the authors' presentation of their empirically grounded theoretical model.

At the other extreme, authors may choose to reserve their integration of existing theory and research with their framework for a discussion section following the results. For example, Gioia and Chittipeddi's (1991) first- and second-order accounts of the sense-making processes involved in the initiation of strategic change do not pose any relationships between elements of their model and other work. That integration takes place in a 'discussion and implications' section of the paper, where the relationship between their theoretical elements and other work is constructed. It is in that section that we find statements like: 'The beginning stage of the overall change effort was perhaps most notable because it involved a cognitive re-orientation or existing interpretive schemes (Bartunek, 1984; Poole et al., 1989; Ranson et al., 1980). A sensible, workable interpretation of a revised organizational reality needed to be proposed and accepted' (Gioia and Chittipeddi, 1991: 444).

The literature that is relevant for various conceptual elements of the developed grounded theory, however, may not be the literature towards which the manuscript's theoretical contribution is directed. For example, the excerpt from Isabella's presentation of the elements that constituted the 'anticipation' phase of her process theory (quoted on p. 118) links her conceptualization to prior work on rumor and gossip. Yet, hers is not a study about rumor but one about interpretive processes during organizational change. That is the theoretical story to which her study proposes to contribute.

Writing contribution: finding and shaping a literature

When we read a published grounded theory study, the case it makes for its having something to contribute to a particular theoretical conversation in management and organization studies is taken for granted as it is part of the fabric of the text. It appears as if researchers had a particular theoretical story in mind from the earliest stages of the study. And, this of course occurs. But, it is also the case that the theoretical conversation to which the composed grounded theory makes a contribution may not be established until after the theoretical frame is developed. Glaser (1978) points out that researchers may not know which literature is relevant until analysis is well advanced. This may even occur during the writing phase as the manuscript is submitted for review and undergoes revision. And, the reviewers and editor may participate in influencing this.

For example, Karen Golden-Biddle tells the story of how a reviewer suggested that she and her co-author consider locating the contribution of their study on a non-profit board in the literature on impression management; they had originally written the manuscript as making a contribution to the literature on institutional theory. Similarly, I had framed the contribution of my study on comedy in medical settings in terms of the literature on organization emotions. The journal editor, however, suggested that the study also had something to say to the literature on service management and proposed that I write its contribution in terms of an intersection between organization emotion and service management.

Writing method

Reading across an over 25-year range of published grounded theory building articles, it is hard not to notice how the requirements for writing method have increased. Following the conventions for writing methods, manuscripts typically provide descriptions of their site and data collection methods as well as of the researchers' analytic operations. While all sections of method appear to have increased, my concern here is with the writing of data analysis. The accounts of analytic process described for example, in Hobbs and Anderson's (1971) study of academic departments and Orlikowski's (1993) investigation into the adoption of case tools stand in stark contrast to each other.

In the former, their analytic operations are described in the following terms:

> On the basis of data concerning the organizational behavior of departmental personnel, a theoretical model of the academic department was developed. Glaser and Strauss's [10, pp. 101–115] 'constant comparative method' for generating theory from data was employed: categories of topics which constituted departmental concerns were constructed from the data gathered in initial interviews; additional data were then collected to permit amendment –

including occasional deletion – and the integration of those categories. Finally, the refined categories were embellished by explanatory categories, also grounded in the data, until the model of the organization of academic departments emerged. (Hobbs and Anderson, 1971: B-135)

In these 91 words, the authors provide their readers with the basic contours of the grounded theory approach they follow, identifying that they took a concept-indicator approach to category development, that they pursued theoretical sampling, and that their categories developed in refinement and generalization.

Compare this with Orlikowski's (1993) account of her analytic operations which occur in two different places in over five and a half pages of 'research methodology.' In the first place, she devotes over 500 words to an overview of the grounded theory approach that details its appropriateness for understanding technology adoption. Then, following a discussion of her research sites and data sources, her data analysis is described through another approximately 700 words. In the journal article, space is a premium, especially for qualitative researchers attempting to take the reader into the social world they studied and to carefully articulate their theoretical points, demonstrating their grounding. What accounts for the apparent increasing allocation of scarce article space to methodological discussions? In no small measure, the answer lies on the one hand in the increasing presence of qualitative manuscripts in our journals and on the other in its readers, particularly those who occupy gatekeeper roles in management and organization publications. The increasing number of qualitative studies brings heightened scrutiny. And, often that scrutiny comes from those researchers who work in the hypothetico-deductive mode. My own sense is that accounts of the analytic process are taking up more journal space because they are trying to accomplish three things: to heighten understanding of the approach used and its potential for developing knowledge, to convince readers that researchers followed procedures associated with good scientific practice, and to increase the transparency of the actual procedures followed.

Writing analysis to heighten understanding of the approach
As Glaser and Strauss (1967), Strauss (1987) and Strauss and Corbin (1990) repeatedly indicate, qualitative work will be read and most likely evaluated by those who use quantitatively based methodologies. While this situation is certainly changing as more and more researchers who pursue qualitative approaches are now editors, editorial board members, and *ad hoc* reviewers, it is still fairly likely that some of the assigned reviewers for a potential grounded theory publication may not be familiar with its logic and research processes. And, given the plurality of qualitative approaches that now constitute the qualitative research

domain described in Chapter 1, the article may be reviewed by qualitative researchers who work from within a different practice domain.

So, clearly researchers are writing to inform readers of the nature of the approach when they write into their methods sections statements like the following:

> First, grounded theory 'is an inductive, theory discovery methodology that allows the researcher to develop a theoretical account of the general features of a topic while simultaneously grounding the account in empirical observations or data' (Martin and Turner, 1986, p. 141). This generative approach seemed particularly useful here given that no change theory of CASE tools adoption and use has been established to date. While models of information technology implementation do exist (Ginzberg, 1981; Lucas, 1978; Markus, 1983) these deal largely with the development stages of IS implementation and focus extensively on user involvement and user relations. As a result, they are less applicable to the issue of organizational change in general, and to the case of CASE tools adoption and use in particular. (Orlikowski, 1993: 310)

The description of the theory building orientation of the approach in the first sentence is then followed by a claim for its particular usefulness when developing currently unavailable models of CASE tool adoption.

Writing analysis to assure good scientific practice was followed
As Karen Golden-Biddle and I noted (1997), one of the issues all researchers face, including those who pursue research through qualitative approaches, is representing themselves as having conducted their investigative work in a manner that comports to the expectations of the conduct of good science. This is a point that Geertz (1988) similarly makes when he emphasizes that authors' ability to get their work read and published hinges on their ability to establish themselves as working within the understood norms of a particular disciplinary community. Writing practices that highlight the researchers' analytic approach as fitting in with the guidelines of good science help to achieve this.

One way in which researchers convey that they are conducting their analysis according to sound scientific practice is through the citing process whereby they invite their readers to see that they are following established practice by referencing prior work. The citation of methodological treatises helps to show procedural authority for research procedures. In the statement 'Analysis of the transcripts involved the identification of common themes, as recommended by Glaser and Strauss (1967) in their description of grounded theory . . .' (Brown and Jones, 1998: 75) the authors' use of the phrase 'as recommended' indicates their comportment with the efforts of others whose work has been vetted by a broader scientific community. A similar move legitimating the approach in terms of prior work is evident in the statement 'Data were collected and analyzed in accordance with guidelines of Glaser and

Strauss (1967), Glaser (1978) and Turner (1981) for the generation of grounded, substantive theory' (Martin, 1984: 173).

While such demonstrations that researchers are following the general contours of the grounded theory building approach are common, expressions of being guided by more specific procedural dimensions are also emphasized. Consequently, Harris and Sutton indicated that they followed specific aspects of established grounded theory procedures in determining the number of informants they should interview. They explained, '[t]he number of informants interviewed for each closing (see Table 1) followed the notion of 'theoretical saturation' suggested by Glaser and Strauss (1967, pp. 61–62); we stopped interviewing additional people when we began hearing the same stories repeated over and over' (1986: 9).

One issue of concern that arises when writing analytic accounts that depict authors as following the norms and practices of the scientific community is the writing of mixed accounts – that is depicting the author as following procedures associated with the hypothetico-deductive as well as the grounded theory building model. For instance, when a study is written as following a random sampling strategy, it invokes the language associated with the former model of research activity. While such language may appeal to reviewers whose experience lies in working with that model, it muddles the procedures associated with the grounded theory building approach. It also invites the expectation that researchers will have followed the procedural conventions associated with testing for statistical generalizability (Elliott et al., 1999). In broader terms, it invites evaluation of the study in terms of hypothetico-deductive criteria rather than those associated with theory building approaches.

Writing analysis to increase transparency of procedures

Most importantly, researchers write their account of the analytic process to provide their readers with insight into the ways in which the conceptual categories and relationships comprising the theoretical framework were composed from data observations. These mean describing the analytic activities in a way such that the reader can readily apprehend what happened. Kahn's (1993) discussion of the analytic strategy he pursued to develop his framework of organizational caregiving illustrates this.

> I derived the behavioral dimensions of caregiving by analyzing agency members' responses to questions in the first interview about the nature of caregiving (i.e. 'What are the behaviors and feelings associated with giving care? With receiving care? What do caring youth volunteer relationships ideally look like?'). I then developed conceptual categories of caregiving behavior from specific behaviors that agency members described. I halted this process only when each instance of a caregiving behavior was adequately accounted for by a conceptual category. (Kahn, 1993: 543)

In this account, Kahn straightforwardly describes how he approached his data documents to derive his conceptual categories and how he exhausted the identified expressions of caregiving to achieve a level of theoretical saturation.

In a development of explicating analytic procedures, researchers are increasingly writing in examples of specific analytic moves, thereby taking their readers imaginatively not only into the investigated research setting but also to their analytic process. Researchers increasingly instance some of their analytic moves. As an illustration, Hargadon and Sutton write:

> Following Glaser & Strauss (1967) and Miles & Huberman (1994) a set of iterations usually began with a hunch inspired by the data or literature (e.g. an informant mentioned that the original idea for a water bottle valve came from another designer who had worked on a previous shampoo bottle project, which suggested that ideas from different industries provided IDEO with potentially valuable solutions in later projects). (1997: 725)

Similarly, in Locke and Golden-Biddle (1997), prompted by a reviewer's request for some examples in the description of our procedures, we illustrate the analytic procedures followed by providing specific instances of analytic moves, such as, 'Finally, we grouped related acts and their practices into categories (Corbin and Strauss, 1990; Strauss and Corbin, 1996); for instance, the textual act of creating discord and the associated practices of making contentious characterizations and dichotomizing were grouped and labeled as "structuring noncoherence (p. 1028)".'

In conclusion, where do I stand on the writing of analytic accounts? Frankly, I would like to see grounded theory building researchers presenting the results of their empirical work doing much less of writing to heighten understanding of the approach and to demonstrate that good scientific practice has been followed. These two dimensions of writing method lend themselves to writing analytical accounts using a rhetoric of justification in which authors are writing from a position in which they have to vindicate their choice of analytic procedure. As I suggested above, journal space is an especially scarce resource for qualitative researchers. Certainly, it is important for qualitative researchers to locate themselves in terms of the approach they are following in a given study and also in terms of the broader school of thought or theoretical perspective that informs their work. But, it does not make sense to give up that space to providing descriptions and justifications of research approaches that are available elsewhere in methodological treatises and that do not add anything substantive to procedural descriptions such that readers can understand the operations followed during analysis. The third, writing for transparency, however, is more likely to result in writing analytic accounts that are in keeping with a rhetoric of explication, than provide those readers who would like to know with a better understanding of how a particular analysis progressed. Such writing would be helpful for others wishing to understand how analysis unfolded through the researchers' major analytic decisions and moves. Some of writing analysis might include the following.

- Identifying researchers' informing school of thought, delineating how it shaped data gathering and analytic activities. Gephart's (1993) discussion of how ethnomethodology directed his attention to the important concepts and language used by organization members during sense-making about disasters (discussed in Chapter 6) provides an illustration of this.
- (Related to the above) delineating how the research questions shaped analysis. For example, Kahn's (1993) presentation of the questions he had in mind as he examined his interview data to discern what constitutes care-giving.
- Noting how major categories emerged by perhaps identifying the events or indicators that first drew researcher attention to these potential categories, as Hargadon and Sutton (1997) did in their discussion (excerpted above) of how the water bottle valve prompted their thinking.
- Describing how theoretical sampling impacted data gathering and analytic procedures. For example, Chapter 6 identified that Coopey et al.'s (1998) analysis of innovation by managers followed two phases: an initial phase of category development followed by a subsequent phase in which the categories composed during the first stage provided the basis for analysis of subsequent interviews.

Concluding comments

I began this book by considering the persistence of grounded theory in studies of organization and management. What accounts for that persistence? I believe there are several relevant considerations. As I noted then, organization and management researchers are by and large schooled in research methods that emphasize a logico-deductive approach executed through quantitative analytic tools. For that audience, the introduction to qualitative methods provided by the original monograph which moves back and forth between the received logico-deductive model and the grounded theory building style of research practice provides a bridge between the two modes of investigation. Its polemical style allows readers to grasp the general logic of the grounded theory approach through its contrast with the model of inquiry to which they have received the most exposure. At the same time as it describes its possibility, the grounded theory approach celebrates the theory generating dimension of scientific activity, and especially the creativity of individual researchers.

Grounded theory provides more than a general logic for conducting qualitative research. It also offers an operational model of the theory building research process and a language with which to articulate it. Terms such as theoretical sampling, theoretical saturation, constant comparative method, theoretical sensitivity, theoretical memos and grounded theory all provide frames of reference from which to think and carry out the work of achieving a theoretical conceptualization of a phenomenon without excessive reliance on prior received theory.

Finally, grounded theory's peculiar mix of subjectivity, interpretivism and science (Denzin, 1988) continues to resonate with and strike a chord amongst a significant group of organizational researchers who are interested in building knowledge from personal experience in categories and terms taken from everyday life. Its concern with interpreting the subjective side of life is broadly appealing. On the other hand, the language that it introduces and uses to describe the research act is one that feels comfortably close to the 'logic of a science that does empirical research' (Denzin, 1988: 431) and the set of discrete procedural steps it outlines similarly reflect such a feel. This combination of science, subjectivity and interpretivism has helped this style of research to be worked from very different paradigmatic stances, as indicated in Chapter one. It is a research approach that travels well to modernist, interpretive and post-modern studies of organization life.

It is quite clear that the account I have provided of grounded theory in the study of organization and management is a sympathetic one. There have been those who have raised legitimate concerns about the approach. For example, some have cautioned against mechanically following grounded theory's operational procedures, because doing so can result in an overemphasis on achieving abstract categories, concepts and patterns at the expense of attaining a full, rich description of the social worlds studied as they are interpreted and understood by those who live and work in them (Denzin, 1988; Ellis, 1992). Others have cautioned against the potential understanding lost by fragmenting data and separating those fragments too quickly from their contexts (Kelle and Laurie, 1995). Such cautions are, of course appropriate, and speak to the need for management researchers to move thoughtfully between operational procedures, experience of organization and work encapsulated in data documents, and theoretical outcomes. When they do so, the grounded theory style of research offers the possibility of creatively exploring dimensions of organizational and managerial life.

References

Agar, M.H. (1980) *The Professional Stranger: An Informal Introduction to Ethnography.* San Diego, CA: Academic Press.

Atkinson, P. and Hammersley, M. (1994) 'Ethnography and participant observation', in N.K. Denzin and Y.S. Lincoln (eds), *Handbook of Qualitative Research.* Thousand Oaks, CA: Sage Publications. pp. 105–17.

Argyris, C. and Schon, D. (1978) *Organizational Learning: A Theory of Action Perspective.* Reading, MA: Addison-Wesley.

Bacharach, S. (1989) 'Organizational theories: some criteria for evaluation', *Academy of Management Review,* **14**, 496–515.

Baker, S. (1983) 'Writing as learning', in P.L. Stock (ed.), *Forum: Essays on Theory and Practice in the Teaching of Writing.* Upper Montclair, NJ: Boynton/Cook. pp. 224–6.

Barburoglu, O.N. and Ravn, I. (1992) 'Normative action research', *Organization Studies,* **13**, 19–34.

Barley, S.R. (1983) 'Semiotics and the study of occupational and organizational culture', *Administrative Science Quarterly,* **28**, 393–413.

Barley, S.R. (1990) 'Images of imaging: notes on doing longitudinal fieldwork', *Organization Science,* **1**, 220–47.

Bartunek, J. (1984) 'Changing interpretive schemes and organizational restructuring: the example of a religious order', *Administrative Science Quarterly,* **29**, 355–72.

Becker, H.S. (1953) 'Becoming a marihuana user', *American Journal of Sociology,* **59**, 235–42.

Becker, H.S. (1958) 'Problems of inference and proof in participant observation', *American Sociological Review,* **23**, 652–60.

Becker, H.S. (1986a) *Doing Things Together: Selected Papers.* Evanston, IL: Northwestern University Press.

Becker, H.S. (1986b) *Writing for Social Scientists: How to Start and Finish Your Thesis, Book, or Article.* Chicago: University of Chicago Press.

Becker, H.S. (1992) 'Cases, causes, conjunctures, stories, and imagery', in C.C. Ragin and H.S. Becker (eds), *What Is a Case?* Cambridge: Cambridge University Press. pp. 217–26.

Becker, H.S., Geer, B., Hughes, E. and Strauss, A.L. (1961) *Boys in White: Student Culture in Medical School.* Chicago: University of Chicago Press.

Berger, P. and Luckman, T.L. (1967) *The Social Construction of Reality.* New York: Doubleday.

Best, S. and Kellner, D. (1997) *The Postmodern Turn.* New York: Guilford Press.

Bigus, O.E., Hadden, S.C. and Glaser, B.G. (1982) 'Basic social processes', in

R.B. Smith and P.K. Manning (eds), *Handbook of Social Science Methods Vol. II, Qualitative Methods*. Cambridge, MA: Ballinger. pp. 251–72.

Blumer, H. (1954) 'What's wrong with social theory?' *American Sociological Review,* **19**, 3–10.

Blumer, H. (1969) *Symbolic Interactionism: Perspective and Method*. Englewood Cliffs, NJ: Prentice Hall.

Blumer, H. (1976) 'The methodological position of symbolic interactionism', in M. Hammersley and P. Woods (eds), *The Process of Schooling*. London: Routledge and Kegan Paul. pp. 12–18.

Boje, D. (1995) 'Stories of the storytelling organization: a postmodern analysis of Disney as "Tamara-Land"', *Academy of Management Journal*, **38**, 997–1035.

Booth, W. (1961) *The Rhetoric of Fiction*. Chicago: University of Chicago Press.

Boyatsis, R.E. (1982) *The Competent Manager: A Model for Effective Performance*. New York: Wiley.

Brown, A. (1998) 'Narrative, politics, and legitimacy in an IT implementation', *Journal of Management Studies*, **35**, 35–58.

Brown, A.D. and Jones, M.R. (1998) 'Doomed to failure: narratives of inevitability and conspiracy in a failed IS project', *Organization Studies*, **19**, 73–88.

Brown, S.L. and Eisenhardt, K.M. (1997) 'The art of continuous change: linking complexity theory and time-paced evolution in relentlessly shifting organizations', *Administrative Science Quarterly*, **42**, 1–34.

Bruner, J. (1991) 'The narrative construction of reality', *Critical Inquiry*, **18**, 1–21.

Bryman, A. (1988) *Quantity and Quality in Social Research*. London: Unwin Hyman.

Bulmer, M. (1988) 'Some reflections upon research in organizations', in A. Bryman (ed.), *Doing Research in Organizations*. London: Routledge. pp. 151–61.

Burgelman, R.A. (1983) 'A process model of internal corporate venturing in the diversified major firm', *Administrative Science Quarterly*, **28**, 223–44.

Burgelman, R.A. (1994) 'Fading memories: A process theory of strategic business exit in dynamic environments', *Administrative Science Quarterly*, **39**, 24–56.

Burgess, R. (1984) *In the Field: An Introduction to Field Research*. London: George Allen and Unwin.

Burke, K. (1969) *A Grammar of Motives*. Berkeley, CA: University of California Press.

Calas, M. (1992) 'An/other silent voice? Representing 'Hispanic woman' in organizational texts', in A.J. Mills and P. Tancred (eds), *Gendering Organization Theory*. Newbury Park, CA: Sage. pp. 201–21.

Calas, M.B. and Smircich, L. (1990) 'Voicing seduction to silence leadership', *Organizational Studies*, **12**, 567–602.

Calas, M.B. and Smircich, L. (1992) 'Rewriting gender into organization theorizing: Directions from feminist perspectives', in M.I. Reed and M.D. Hughes (eds), *Re-thinking Organization: New Directions in Organizational Research and Analysis*. London: Sage Publications. pp. 227–53.

Charmaz, K. (1990) '"Discovering" chronic illness: Using grounded theory', *Sociology of Health and Ilness*, **30**, 1161–72.

Chenitz, W.C. (1986) 'The informal interview', in W.C. Chenitz and J.M. Swanson (eds), *From Practice to Grounded Theory: Qualitative Research in Nursing*. Menlo-Park, CA: Addison Wesley. pp. 79–90.

Chenitz W.C. and Swanson, J.M. (1986) 'Qualitative research using grounded theory', in W.C. Chenitz and J.M. Swanson (eds), *From Practice to Grounded Theory: Qualitative Research in Nursing*. Menlo-Park, CA: Addison-Wesley. pp. 3–15.

Coch, L. and French, J.R. (1948) 'Overcoming resistance to change', *Human Relations*, **1**, 512–32.

Cohen, M., March, J. and Olsen, J. (1972) 'A garbage-can model of organizational choice', *Administrative Science Quarterly*, **17**, 1–25.

Cohen, M.Z. (1987) A historical overview of the phenomenologic movement. *Image: Journal of Nursing Scholarship*, **19**, 31–34.

Collins, R. and Makowsky, M. (1978) *The Discovery of Society*. New York: Random House.

Coopey, J., Keegan, O. and Emler, N. (1998) 'Managers' innovations and the structuration of organizations', *Journal of Management Studies*, **35**, 264–84.

Corbin, J. (1986) 'Qualitative data analysis for grounded theory', in W.C. Chenitz and J.M. Swanson (eds), *From Practice to Grounded Theory: Qualitative Research in Nursing*. Menlo-Park, CA: Addison Wesley. pp. 91–101.

Corbin, J. (1991) 'Anselm Strauss: an intellectual biography', in D. Maines (ed.), *Social Organization and Social Process: Essays in Honor of Anselm Strauss*. New York: Aldine De Gruyter. pp. 17–42.

Corbin, J. and Strauss, A.L. (1990) 'Grounded theory method: Procedures, canons, and evaluative criteria', *Qualitative Sociology*, **13**, 3–21.

Covaleski, M.A., Dirsmith, M.A., Heian, J.B. and Samuel, S. (1998) 'The calculated and the avowed: techniques of discipline and struggles over identity in big six public accounting firms', *Administrative Science Quarterly*, **43**, 293–327.

Coyne, I.T. (1997) 'Sampling in qualitative research. Purposeful and theoretical sampling; merging or clear boundaries?', *Journal of Advanced Nursing*, **26**, 623–30.

Cressey, D. (1932) *The Taxi Dance Hall*. Chicago: University of Chicago Press.

Cunliffe, A. (2000) Reflexive inquiry. Working Paper.

Cunliffe, A. (2000b) 'Managers as practical authors: Reconstructing our understanding of management practice', *Journal of Management Studies*.

Czarniawska, B. and Joerges, B. (1996) 'Travels of ideas', in B. Czarniawska and G. Sevon (eds), *Translating Organizational Change*. Berlin: Walter de Gruyter. pp. 13–48.

Denzin, N. (1988) 'Qualitative Analysis for Social Scientists: Book Review', *Contemporary Sociology*, **17**, 430–32.

Denzin, N. (1989a) *The Research Act: A Theoretical Introduction to Sociological Methods* (3rd Edn). Englewood Cliffs, NJ: Prentice Hall.

Denzin, N. (1989b) *Interpretive Interactionism*. Newbury Park, CA: Sage.

Denzin, N. (1992) *Symbolic Interactionism and Cultural Studies*. Cambridge: Basil Blackwell.

Denzin, N. (1994) 'The art and politics of interpretation', in N.K. Denzin and Y.S. Lincoln (eds), *Handbook of Qualitative Research*. Thousand Oaks, CA: Sage. pp. 500–15.

Denzin, N. and Lincoln, Y.S. (1994) *Handbook of Qualitative Research*. Thousand Oaks, CA: Sage.

Derrida, J. (1976) *Of Grammatology*. Baltimore, MD: Johns Hopkins University Press.

Derrida, J. (1978) *Writing and Difference*. London: Routledge.

DiMaggio, P.J. (1995) 'Comments on "what theory is not"', *Administrative Science Quarterly*, **40**, 391–7.

Dowst, K. (1980) 'The epistemic approach: writing, knowing and learning', in T. Donovan and B. McClelland (eds), *Eight Approaches to Teaching Composition*. Urbana, IL: National Council of Teachers of English. pp. 65–85.

Dunn, W.N. and Swierczek, F.W. (1977) 'Planned organization change: toward grounded theory', *The Journal of Applied Behavioral Science*, **13**, 136–57.

Easterby-Smith, M., Thorpe, R. and Lowe, A. (1991) *Management Research: An introduction*. London: Sage.

Eco, U. (1976) *A Theory of Semiotics*. Bloomington, IN: University of Indiana Press.

Eisenhardt, K.M. (1989a) 'Making fast strategic decisions in high velocity environments', *Academy of Management Journal*, **32**, 543–76.

Eisenhardt, K. M. (1989b) 'Building theories from case study research', *Academy of Management Review*, **14**, 532–50.

Eisenhardt, K.M. and Bourgeois, L.J. (1988) 'Politics of strategic decision-making in high velocity environments: toward a midrange theory', *Academy of Management Journal*, **31**, 737–70.

Elbow, P. (1981) *Writing with Power: Techniques for Mastering the Writing Process*. Oxford University Press.

Elden, M. and Chisolm, R. (1993) 'Emerging varieties of action research: Introduction to the special issue', *Human Relations*, **46**, 121–42.

Elliott, R., Fischer, C.T. and Rennie, D.L. (1999) 'Evolving guidelines for publication of qualitative research studies in psychology and related fields', *British Journal of Clinical Psychology*, **38**, 215–29.

Ellis, C. (1992) 'Basics of grounded theory: Book review', *Contemporary Sociology*, **21**, 138–9.

Ellis, C. and Bochner, A.P. (eds) (1996) *Composing Ethnography: Alternative Forms of Qualitative Writing*. Walnut Creek, CA: Altmira Press.

Elsbach, K.D., Sutton, R.I. and Whetten, D.I. (1999) 'Perspectives on developing management theory, circa 1999: moving from shrill monologues to (relatively) tame dialogues', *Academy of Management Review*, **24**, 627–33.

Emig, J. (1977) 'Writing as a mode of learning', *College Composition and Communication*, **25**, 122–8.

Fetterman, D.M. (1998) 'Ethnography', in L. Bickman and D.J. Rog (eds), *Handbook of Applied Social Research Methods*. Thousand Oaks, CA: Sage. pp. 473–504.

Fox-Wolfgramm, S.J. (1997) 'Toward developing a methodology for doing qualitative research: the dynamic-comparative case study method', *Scandinavian Journal of Management*, **13**, 439–57.

Fox-Wolfgramm, S.J., Boal, K.B. and Hunt, J.G. (1998) 'Organizational adaptation to institutional change: a comparative study of first-order change in prospector and defender banks', *Administrative Science Quarterly*, **43**, 87–126.

Garfinkle, H. (1967) *Studies in Ethnomethodology*. Cambridge: Polity.

Geertz, C. (1973) *The Interpretation of Cultures*. New York: Basic Books.

Geertz, C. (1988) *Works and Lives: The Anthropologist as Author*. Stanford, CA: Stanford University Press.

Gephart, R.P. (1978) 'Status degradation and organizational succession: an ethnomethodological approach', *Administrative Science Quarterly*, **23**, 553–81.

Gephart, R.P. (1993) 'The textual approach: risk and blame in disaster sense-making', *Academy of Management Journal*, **36**, 1465–514.

Gersick, C.J. (1988) 'Time and transition in work teams: toward a new model of group development', *Academy of Management Journal*, **31**, 9–41.

Glaser, B.G. (1964) 'Awareness contexts and social interaction', *American Sociological Review*, **29**, 669–79.

Glaser, B.G. (1965) 'The constant comparative method of qualitative analysis', *Social Problems*, **12**, 436–45.

Glaser, B.G. (1978) *Theoretical Sensitivity*. Mill Valley, CA: Sociology Press.

Glaser, B.G. (1992) *Basics of Grounded Theory Analysis*. Mill Valley, CA: Sociology Press.

Glaser, B.G. (1998) *Doing Grounded Theory: Issues and Discussions*. Mill Valley, CA: Sociology Press.

Glaser, B.G. and Strauss, A.L. (1964) 'Awareness contexts and social interaction', *American Sociological Review*, **29**, 669–79.

Glaser, B.G. and Strauss, A.L. (1965a) 'Temporal aspects of dying as a non-scheduled status passage', *American Journal of Sociology*, **71**, 48–59.

Glaser, B.G. and Strauss, A.L. (1965b) *Awareness of Dying*. Chicago: Aldine.

Glaser, B.G. and Strauss, A. L. (1967) *The Discovery of Grounded Theory*. Chicago: Aldine.

Glaser, B.G. and Strauss, A. L. (1968) *A Time for Dying*. Chicago: Aldine.

Goia, D. and Chittipeddi, K. (1991) 'Sensemaking and sensegiving in strategic change initiation', *Strategic Management Journal*, **12**, 433–48.

Golden-Biddle, K. and Locke, K. (1993) 'Appealing work: an investigation of how ethnographic texts convince', *Organization Science*, **4**, 595–616.

Golden-Biddle, K. and Locke, K. (1997) *Composing Qualitative Research*. Thousand Oaks, CA: Sage.

Gould, S.J. (1993) 'Fulfilling the spandrels of world and mind', in J. Selzer (ed.), *Understanding Scientific Prose*. Madison, WI: The University of Wisconsin Press. pp. 310–36.

Grant, L. and Fine, G.A. (1992) 'Creative directions in classical ethnography', in M.D. LeCompte, W.L. Millroy and J. Preissle (eds), *The Handbook of Qualitative Research in Education*. San Diego, CA: Academic Press. pp. 405–47.

Guba, E.G. and Lincoln, Y.S. (1994) 'Competing paradigms in qualitative research', in N.K. Denzin and Y.S. Lincoln (eds), *Handbook of Qualitative Research*. Thousand Oaks, CA: Sage. pp. 105–17.

Gummesson, E. (1991) *Qualitative Methods in Management Research*, 2nd Edn. Newbury Park, CA: Sage.

Hammersley, M. and Atkinson, P. (1983) *Ethnography: Principles in Practice*. London: Tavistock.

Hardy, C. and Palmer, I. (1999) 'Pedagogical practice and postmodernist ideas', *Journal of Management Education*, **23**, 377–95.

Hargadon, A. and Sutton, R.I. (1997) 'Technology brokering and innovation in a product development firm', *Administrative Science Quarterly*, **42**, 716–49.

Harris, S.G. and Sutton, R.I. (1986) 'Functions of parting ceremonies in dying organizations', *Academy of Management Journal*, **29**, 5–30.

Hassard, J. (1990) 'An alternative to paradigm incommensurability in organization theory', in J. Hassard and D. Pym (eds), *The Theory and Philosophy of Organizations*. London: Routledge. pp. 219–30.

Hatch, M.J. (1997) *Organization Theory: Modern, Symbolic, and Postmodern Perspectives.* Oxford University Press.

Hawk, T.F. (1991) Collateral/parallel organizing for strategic change. Doctoral dissertation, University of Pittsburgh.

Henwood, K.L. and Pidgeon, N.F. (1995) 'Remaking the link: qualitative research and feminist standpoint theory', *Feminism and Psychology,* 5, 7–30.

Hobbs, W.C. and Anderson, G.L. (1971) 'The operation of academic departments', *Management Science,* 18, B-134–B-144.

Hodder, I. (1994) 'The interpretation of documents and material culture', in N.K. Denzin and Y.S. Lincoln (eds), *Handbook of Qualitative Research.* Thousand Oaks, CA: Sage. pp. 393–402.

Human Relations (1993) Emerging varieties of action research. *Human Relations,* 46(2).

Inkpen, A.C. and Dinur, A. (1998) 'Knowledge management processes and international joint ventures', *Organization Science,* 9, 454–70.

Isabella, L.A. (1990) 'Evolving interpretations as a change unfolds: how managers construe key organizational events', *Academy of Management Journal,* 33, 7–41.

Iser, W. (1978) *The Act of Reading: A Theory of Aesthetic Response.* Baltimore, MD: Johns Hopkins University Press.

Iser, W. (1989) *Prospecting: From Reader Response to Literary Anthropology.* Baltimore, MD: Johns Hopkins University Press.

Kahn, W.A. (1993) 'Caring for the caregivers: patterns of organizational caregiving', *Administrative Science Quarterly,* 38, 539–63.

Keddy, B., Sims, S.L. and Stern, P.N. (1996) 'Grounded theory as feminist research methodology', *Journal of Advanced Nursing,* 23, 448–53.

Kelle, U. and Laurie, H. (1995) 'Computer use in qualitative research and issues of validity', in U. Kelle (ed.) *Computer-aided Qualitative Data Analysis.* London: Sage. pp. 19–28.

Kilduff, M. (1993) 'Deconstructing organizations', *Academy of Management Review,* 18, 13–31.

Kincheloe, J.L. and McLaren, P.L. (1994) 'Rethinking critical theory and qualitative research', in N.K. Denzin and Y.S. Lincoln (eds), *Handbook of Qualitative Research.* Thousand Oaks, CA: Sage. pp. 138–57.

Knorr-Cetina, K. (1981) *The Manufacture of Knowledge: An Essay on the Constructivist and Contextual Nature of Science.* New York: Pergamon Press.

Konecki, K. (1997) 'Time in the recruiting search process by headhunting companies', in A.L. Strauss and J. Corbin (eds), *Grounded Theory in Practice.* Thousand Oaks, CA: Sage. pp. 131–46.

Kram, K.E. (1983) 'Phases of the mentoring relationship', *Academy of Management Journal,* 26, 608–25.

Kram, K.E. and Isabella, L.A. (1985) 'Mentoring alternatives: the role of peer relationships in career development', *Academy of Management Journal,* 28, 110–32.

Kuhn, T.S. (1970) *The Structure of Scientific Revolutions,* 2nd Edn. Chicago: University of Chicago Press.

Kunda, G. (1991) *Engineering Culture: Culture and Control in a High Tech Organization.* Philadelphia, PA: Temple University.

Langley, A. (1999) 'Strategies of theorizing from process data', *Academy of Management Review,* 24, 691–710.

Laurila, J. (1997) 'Promoting research access and informant rapport in corporate settings: notes from research on a crisis company', *Scandinavian Journal of Management*, **13**, 407–18.

Lawrence, P.R. (1981) 'The Harvard organization and environment program', in A.H. Van de Ven and W.F. Joyce (eds), *Perspectives on Organization Design and Behavior*. New York: Wiley. pp. 311–37.

Lawrence, P.R. and Lorsch, J.W. (1967) *Organization and Environment: Managing differentiation and integration*. Cambridge, Mass: Harvard University Press.

Layder, D. (1990) *The Realist Image in Social Science*. New York: St. Martin Press.

Layder, D. (1994) *Understanding Social Theory*. London: Sage.

LeCompte, M.D., Millroy, W.L. and Preissle, J. (1993) 'Introduction', in M.D. LeCompte, W.L. Millroy and J. Preissle (eds), *The Handbook of Qualitative Research in Education*. San Diego, CA: Academic Press. pp. xix–xxxvi.

Lee, M.D., MacDermid, S.M. and Buck, M.L. (In press) 'Organizational paradigms of reduced load work: accommodation, elaboration, transformation', *Academy of Management Journal*.

Lewin, K. (1951) *Field Theory in Social Science*. New York: Harper & Row.

Linstead, S. (1993) 'From postmodern anthropology to deconstructive ethnography', *Human Relations*, **46**, 97–120.

Locke, K. (1996) 'A funny thing happened! The management of consumer emotions in service encounters', *Organization Science*, **7**, 40–59.

Locke, K. (1997) 'Re-writing the discovery of grounded theory after 25 years?', *Journal of Management Inquiry*, **5**, 239–45.

Locke, K. and Brazelton, J. (1997) 'Why do we ask them to write, or whose writing is it, anyway', *Journal of Management Education*, **21**, 44–57.

Locke, K. and Golden-Biddle, K. (1997) 'Constructing opportunities for contribution: structuring intertextual coherence and problematizing in organization studies', *Academy of Management Journal*, **40**, 1023–62.

Lofland, J. and Lofland, L. (1984) *Analyzing Social Settings: A Guide to Qualitative Observation and Analysis*, 2nd Edn. Belmont, CA: Wadsworth.

Lonkila, M. (1995) 'Grounded theory as an emerging paradigm for computer-assisted qualitative data analysis', in U. Kelle (ed.) *Computer-aided Qualitative Data Analysis*. London: Sage. pp. 41–51.

Lowenberg, J.S. (1993) 'Interpretive research methodology: broadening the dialogue', *Advances in Nursing Science*, **16**, 57–69.

Lyles, M.A. and Mitroff, I.I. (1980) 'Organizational problem formulation: an empirical study', *Administrative Science Quarterly*, **25**, 102–19.

Maines, D. (1991) 'Reflections, framings, and appreciations', in D. Maines (ed.), *Social Organization and Social Process: Essays in Honor of Anselm Strauss*. New York: Aldine De Gruyter. pp. 3–10.

Malinowski, B. (1922) *Argonauts of the Western Pacific*. New York: E.P. Dutton.

Manning, P.K. (1987) *Semiotics and Fieldwork*. Newbury Park, CA: Sage.

Manning, P.K. (1992) *Organizational Communication*. New York: Aldine de Gruyter.

Martin, J. (1990) 'Deconstructing organizational taboos: the suppression of gender conflict in organizations', *Organization Science*, **1**, 339–59.

Martin, P.Y. (1984) 'Trade unions, conflict and the nature of work in residential service organizations', *Organization Studies*, **5**, 169–85.

Martin, P.Y. and Turner, B.A. (1986) 'Grounded theory and organizational research', *The Journal of Applied Behavioral Science*, **22**, 141–57.

Maxwell, J.A. (1998) 'Designing a qualitative study', in L. Bickman and D.J. Rog (eds), *Handbook of Applied Social Research Methods*. Thousand Oaks, CA: Sage. pp. 69–100.

McCracken, G. (1988) 'The long interview', in *Qualitative Research Methods*, Vol. 13. Newbury Park, CA: Sage.

McCrimmon, J.M. (1976) 'Writing as a way of knowing', in R.L. Graves (ed.), *Rhetoric and Composition: A Source Book for Teachers and Writers*. Upper Montclair, NJ: Boynton/Cook. pp. 3–12

Mead, G.H. (1934) *Mind, Self and Society*. Chicago: University of Chicago Press.

Mead, M. (1928) *Coming of Age in Samoa*. New York: Morrow.

Meltzer, B., Petras, J. and Reynolds, L (1975) *Symbolic Interactionism*. London: Routledge.

Merton, R.K. (1987) 'Three fragments from a sociologist's notebook: establishing the phenomenon, specified ignorance, and strategic research materials', *Annual Review of Sociology*, **13**, 1–28.

Miles, M.B. (1979) 'Qualitative data as attractive nuisance: the problem of analysis', *Administrative Science Quarterly*, **25**, 580–9.

Miles, M.B. and Huberman, A.M. (1984) *Qualitative Data Analysis*. Thousand Oaks, CA: Sage.

Miles, M.B. and Huberman, A.M. (1994) *Qualitative Data Analysis*, 2nd Edn. Thousand Oaks, CA: Sage.

Mintzberg, H. (1973) *The Nature of Managerial Work*. New York: Harper and Row.

Mintzberg, H. (1979) 'An emerging strategy of "direct" research', *Administrative Science Quarterly*, **24**, 582–9.

O'Connor, E.S. (1996) 'Telling decisions: the role of narrative in organizational decision making', in Z. Shapira (ed.), *Organizational Decision Making*. Oxford University Press. pp. 304–23.

Orlikowski, W. (1993) 'Case tools as organizational change: investigating incremental and radical changes in systems development', *MIS Quarterly*, **17**, 309–41.

Orton, J.D. (1997) 'From inductive to iterative grounded theory: zipping the gap between process theory and process data', *Scandinavian Journal of Management*, **13**, 419–38.

Paget, M.A. (1995) 'Performing the text', in J. Van Maanen (ed.), *Representation in Ethnography*. Thousand Oaks, CA: Sage. pp. 222–44.

Pandit, N.R. (1996) 'The creation of theory: a recent application of the grounded theory method', *The Qualitative Report, Online at http://www.nova.edu/sss/QR/QR2–4/Pandit.html* [1999, February 2].

Parker, M. (1992) 'Post-modern organizations or postmodern organization theory?', *Organization Studies*, **13**, 1–17.

Parry, K.W. (1998) 'Grounded theory and social process: a new direction for leadership research', *Leadership Quarterly*, **9**, 85–106.

Partington, D. (2000) 'Building grounded theories of managerial action', *British Journal of Management*, **11**, 91–102.

Patton, M.Q. (1981) *Creative Evaluation*. Beverly Hills, CA: Sage.

Patton, M.Q. (1987) *How to Use Qualitative Methods in Evaluation*. Newbury Park, CA: Sage.

Patton, M.Q. (1990) *Qualitative Evaluation and Research Methods*, 2nd Edn. Newbury Park, CA: Sage.

Pentland, B.T. (1999) 'Building process theory with narrative: from description to explanation', *Academy of Management Review,* **24**, 711–24.

Pettigrew, A.M. (1990) 'Longitudinal field research on change: theory and practice', *Organization Science,* **1**, 267–92.

Pettigrew, A.M. (1997) 'What is a processual analysis?', *Scandinavian Journal of Management,* **13**, 337–48.

Pfeffer, J. (1993) 'Barriers to the development of organization science: paradigm development as a dependent variable', *Academy of Management Review,* **18**, 599–620.

Phillips, N. and Brown, J.L. (1993) 'Analyzing communication in and around organizations: A critical hermeneutic approach', *Academy of Management Journal,* **36**, 1547–76.

Pidgeon, N.F., Turner, B.A. and Blockley, D.I. (1991) 'The use of grounded theory for conceptual analysis in knowledge elicitation', *International Journal of Man – Machine Studies,* **35**, 151–73.

Poole, P.P. (1998) 'Words and deeds of organizational change', *Journal of Managerial Issues,* **10**, 45–59.

Post, J.E. and Andrews, P.N. (1982) 'Case research in corporation and society studies', *Research In Corporate Social Performance and Policy,* **4**, 1–33.

Prasad, P. (1993) 'Symbolic processes in the implementation of technological change: a symbolic interactionist study of work computerization', *Academy of Management Journal,* **36**, 1400–29.

Pratt, M.G. and Rafaeli, A. (1997) 'Organizational dress as a symbol of multi-layered social identities', *Academy of Management Journal,* **40**, 862–98.

Prus, R. (1996) *Symbolic Interaction and Ethnographic Research: Intersubjectivity and the Study of Human Lived Experience.* Albany, NY: State University of New York Press.

Pugh, D. (1988) 'The Aston research programme', in A. Bryman (ed.), *Doing Research in Organizations.* London: Routledge. pp. 123–35.

Rabinow, P. and Sullivan, W. (1979) 'The interpretive turn: a second look', in P. Rabinow and W. Sullivan (eds), *Interpretive Social Science: A Second Look.* Berkeley, CA: University of California Press. pp. 1–30.

Rafaeli, A. and Sutton, R.I. (1991) 'Emotional contrast strategies as means of social influence: lessons from criminal interrogators and bill collectors' *Academy of Management Journal,* **34**, 749–75.

Ragin, C.C. (1992) 'Introduction: cases of "what is a case?"', in C.C. Ragin and H.S. Becker (eds), *What is a Case? Exploring the Foundations of Social Inquiry.* Cambridge University Press. pp. 1–18.

Reason, P. (1988) *Human Inquiry in Action.* London: Sage.

Reason, P. (1994) 'Three approaches to participative inquiry', in N.K. Denzin and Y.S. Lincoln (eds), *Handbook of Qualitative Research.* Thousand Oaks, CA: Sage. pp. 324–39.

Reason, P. and Heron, J. (1986) 'Research with people: the paradigm of experiential co-operative inquiry', *Person Centered Review,* **1**, 456–75.

Reeves, T.K. and Turner, B.A. (1972) 'A theory of organization in batch production factories', *Administrative Science Quarterly,* **17**, 81–98.

Reis Louis, M. (1977) 'How individuals conceptualize conflict: identification of steps in the process and the role of personal/developmental factors', *Human Relations,* **30**, 451–67.

Rennie, D.L. (1998) 'Grounded theory methodology: the pressing need for a coherent logic of justification', *Theory and Psychology*, **8**, 101–20.

Rennie, D.L. (2000) 'Grounded theory methodology as methodical hermeneutics: reconciling, realism and relativism', *Theory and Psychology*, **10**, 481–502.

Richardson, L. (1995) 'Narrative and sociology', in J. Van Maanen (ed.), *Representation in Ethnography*. Thousand Oaks, CA: Sage. pp. 198–221.

Rock, P. (1979) *The Making of Symbolic Interactionism*. London: Macmillan.

Ropo, A., Eriksson, P. and Hunt, J.G. (1997) 'Reflections on conducting processual research on management and organizations', *Scandinavian Journal of Management*, **13**, 331–6.

Rorty, R. (1982) *The Consequences of Pragmatism*. Minneapolis, MN: University of Minnesota Press.

Rosaldo, R. (1989) *Culture and Truth: The Remaking of Social Analysis*. Boston, MA: Bacon.

Ross, J. and Staw, B.M. (1993) 'Organizational escalation and exit: lessons from the Shoreham nuclear power plant', *Academy of Management Journal*, **36**, 701–32.

Rubin, H. and Rubin, I. (1995) *Qualitative Interviewing: The Art of Hearing Data*. Thousand Oaks, CA: Sage.

Schatzman, L. (1991) 'Dimensional analysis: notes on an alternative approach to the grounding of theory in qualitative research', in D.R. Maines (ed.), *Social Organization and Social Process: Essays in Honor of Anselm Strauss*. New York: Aldine de Gruyter. pp. 303–14.

Schatzman, L. and Strauss, A.I. (1973) *Field Research: Strategies for a Natural Sociology*, Englewood Cliffs, NJ: Prentice Hall.

Schwandt, T.A. (1994) 'Constructivist, interpretivist approaches to human inquiry', in N.K. Denzin and Y.S. Lincoln (eds), *Handbook of Qualitative Research*. Thousand Oaks, CA: Sage. pp. 118–37.

Selzer, J. (1993) *Understanding Scientific Prose*. Madison, WI: University of Wisconscin Press.

Shaw, C.R. (1930) *The Jack-Roller: A Delinquent Boy's Own Story*. Chicago: University of Chicago Press.

Singh, V. (1999) Exploring male and female managers perspectives on the meaning and assessment of commitment: cases from leading British and Swedish engineering companies. Doctoral dissertation, Cranfield School of Management.

Spector, M. and Kitsuse, J.I. (1977) *Constructing Social Problems*. Redwood City, CA: Benjamin Cummings.

Spradley, J.P. (1979) *The Ethnographic Interview*. New York: Holt, Rinehart and Winston.

Spradley, J.P. (1980) *Participant Observation*. New York: Holt, Rinehart, and Winston.

Stake, R.E. (1994) 'Case studies', in N.K. Denzin and Y.S. Lincoln (eds), *Handbook of Qualitative Research*. Thousand Oaks, CA: Sage. pp. 236–47.

Stake, R.E. (1995) *The Art of Case Study Research*. Thousand Oaks: CA: Sage.

Stanley, L. and Wise, S. (1983) *Breaking out: Feminist Consciousness and Feminist Research*. London: Routledge and Kegan Paul.

Star, S.L. (1991) 'The sociology of the invisible: the primacy of work in the writings of Anselm Strauss', in D.R. Maines (ed.), *Social Organization and Social*

Process: Essays in Honor of Anselm Strauss. New York: Aldine De Gruyter. pp. 265–84.

Stern, P.N. (1994) 'Eroding grounded theory', in J.M. Morse (ed.), *Critical Issues in Qualitative Research Methods.* Thousand Oaks, CA: Sage. pp. 212–23.

Strauss, A.L. (1970) 'Discovering new theory from previous theory', in T. Shibutani (ed.), *Human Nature and Collective Theory: PAGES.* Englewood Cliffs, NJ: Prentice Hall.

Strauss, A.L. (1987) *Qualitative Analysis for Social Scientists.* Cambridge University Press.

Strauss, A.L. and Corbin, J. (1990) *Basics of Qualitative Research: Grounded Theory Procedures and Techniques.* Thousand Oaks, CA: Sage.

Strauss, A.L. and Corbin, J. (1994) 'Grounded theory methodology: an overview', in J.S. Lincoln (ed.), *Handbook of Qualitative Research.* Thousand Oaks, CA: Sage. pp. 273–86.

Strauss, A.L. and Corbin, J. (1998) *Basics of Qualitative Research: Techniques and Procedures for Developing Grounded Theory,* 2nd Edn. Thousand Oaks, CA: Sage.

Susman, G.I. and Evered, R.D. (1978) 'An assessment of the scientific merits of action research', *Administrative Science Quarterly,* **23**, 582–603.

Sutton, R.I. (1987) 'The process of organizational death: disbanding and reconnecting', *Administrative Science Quarterly,* **32**, 542–69.

Sutton, R.I. and Callahan, A.L. (1987) 'The stigma of bankruptcy: spoiled organizational image and its management', *Academy of Management Journal,* **30**, 405–36.

Sutton, R.I. and Staw, B.M. (1995) 'What theory is not', *Administrative Science Quarterly,* **40**, 371–84.

Swanson, J.M. (1986a) 'The formal qualitative interview for grounded theory', in W.C. Chenitz and J.M. Swanson (eds), *From Practice to Grounded Theory: Qualitative Research in Nursing.* Menlo-Park, CA: Addison-Wesley. pp. 65–78.

Swanson, J.M. (1986b) 'Analyzing data for categories and description', in W.C. Chenitz and J.M. Swanson (eds), *From Practice to Grounded Theory: Qualitative Research in Nursing.* Menlo Park, CA: Addison-Wesley. pp. 121–32.

Thomas, H. (1993) 'Interviewing important people in big companies', *Journal of Contemporary Ethnography,* **22**, 80–96.

Thomas, W.I. and Znaniecki, F. (1918) *The Polish Peasant in Europe and America.* New York: Dover.

Turner, B.A. (1976) 'The organizational and interorganizational development of disasters', *Administrative Science Quarterly,* **21**, 378–97.

Turner, B.A. (1978) *Man-made Disasters.* London: Wykeham Press.

Turner, B.A. (1981) 'Some practical aspects of qualitative data analysis: one way of organising the cognitive processes associated with the generation of grounded theory', *Quality and Quantity,* **15**, 225–47.

Turner, B.A. (1983) 'The use of grounded theory for the qualitative analysis of organizational behavior', *Journal of Management Studies,* **20**, 333–47.

Turner, B.A. (1988) 'Connoisseurship in the study of organizational cultures', in A. Bryman (ed.), *Doing Research in Organizations.* London: Routledge. pp. 108–22.

Van Maanen, J. (1979) 'The fact of fiction in organizational ethnography', *Administrative Science Quarterly,* **24**, 539–50.

Van Maanen, J. (1988) *Tales of the Field: On Writing Ethnography.* Chicago: University of Chicago Press.

Van Maanen, J. (1995) 'An end to innocence: the ethnography of ethnography', in J. Van Maanen (ed.), *Representation in Ethnography.* Thousand Oaks, CA: Sage. pp. 1–35.

Van Maanen, J. (1998) Workshop on ethnographic research. Presented at the Academy of Management Conference, Research Methods Division, San Diego, CA.

Vaughan, D. (1983) *Controlling Unlawful Organizational Behavior: Social Structure and Corporate Misconduct.* Chicago: University of Chicago Press.

Vaughan, D. (1992) 'Theory elaboration: the heuristics of case analysis', in C.C. Ragin and H.S. Becker (eds), *What is a Case: Exploring the Foundations of Social Inquiry.* Cambridge University Press. pp. 173–202.

Vidich, A.J. and Lyman, S.M. (1994) 'Qualitative methods: their history in sociology and anthropology', in N.K. Denzin and Y.S. Lincoln (eds), *Handbook of Qualitative Research.* Thousand Oaks, CA: Sage. pp. 23–59.

Wax, M. (1972) 'Tenting with Malinowski', *American Sociological Review*, **37**, 1–13.

Weick, K.E. (1969) *The Social Psychology of Organizing.* Reading, MA: Addison-Wesley.

Weick, K.E. (1995) 'What theory is not, theorizing is', *Administrative Science Quarterly*, **40**, 385–90.

Weick, K.E. (1999) 'Theory construction as disciplined reflexivity: tradeoffs in the 90s', *Academy of Management Review*, **24**, 797–806.

Whetton, A. (1989) 'What constitutes a theoretical contribution?', *Academy of Management Review*, **14**, 490–5.

Whyte, W.F. (1955) *Street Corner Society: The Social Structure of an Italian Slum*, 3rd Edn. Chicago: University of Chicago Press.

Whyte, W.F. (1984) *Learning from the Field: A Guide from Experience.* Beverly Hills, CA: Sage.

Whyte, W.F. (1991) *Social Theory for Action.* Newbury Park, CA: Sage.

Wilson, H.K. and Hutchinson, S.A. (1996) 'Methodologic mistakes in grounded theory', *Nursing Research*, **45**, 122–4.

Winsor, D. (1993) 'Constructing scientific knowledge in Gould and Lewontin's "The spandrels of San Marco"', in J. Selzer (ed.), *Understanding Scientific Prose.* Madison, WI: University of Wisconsin Press. pp. 127–43.

Wolcott, H.F. (1980) 'How to look like an anthropologist without being one', *Practicing Anthropology*, **3**, 56–9.

Wolcott, H.F. (1992) 'Posturing in qualitative research', in M.D. LeCompte, W.L. Millroy and J. Preissle (eds), *The Handbook of Qualitative Research in Education.* San Diego, CA: Academic Press. pp. 3–52.

Woods, P. (1992) 'Symbolic interactionism: theory and method', in M.D. LeCompte, W.L. Millroy and J. Preissle (eds), *The Handbook of Qualitative Research in Education.* San Diego, CA: Academic Press. pp. 337–404.

Yan, A. and Gray, B. (1994) 'Bargaining power: management control and performance in United States–China joint ventures – A comparative case study', *Academy of Management Journal*, **37**, 1478–1517.

Yearley, S. (1981) 'Textual persuasion: the role of social accounting in the construction of scientific arguments', *Philosophy of Social Science*, **11**, 409–35.

Yin, R.K. (1981) 'The case study crisis: some answers', *Administrative Science Quarterly*, **26**, 58–65.

Yin, R.K. (1984) *Case Study Research*. Beverly Hills, CA: Sage.

Yin, R.K. (1994) *Case Study Research*, 2nd Edn. Thousand Oaks, CA: Sage.

Yin, R.K. (1998) 'The abridged version of case study research: design and method', in L. Bickman and D.J. Rog (eds), *Handbook of Applied Social Research Methods*. Thousand Oaks, CA: Sage. pp. 229–60.

Zbaracki, M.J. (1998) 'The rhetoric and reality of total quality management', *Administrative Science Quarterly*, **43**, 602–36.

Index